Chasing Bones

An Archaeologist's Pursuit of Skeletons

Rachel K. Wentz

Chasing Bones
An Archaeologist's Pursuit of Skeletons

Photographs, including cover, are by the author unless otherwise noted.

ISBN 10: 1-886104-46-8
ISBN 13: 978-1-886104-46-4

The Florida Historical Society Press
435 Brevard Avenue
Cocoa, FL 32922
www.myfloridahistory.org/fhspress

P•R•E•S•S

For my parents, who missed all of this.

Table of Contents

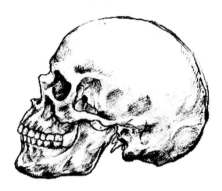

Preface

Walking Away

Today I walk away from my life. I've spent the last thirteen years as a firefighter/paramedic, working among the congested streets of Orlando, Florida, where I've treated an endless array of patients and conditions. From transients to tourists, shootings to stabbings, hangings to hangnails, this job has provided an endless landscape of human drama, played out on the streets of the city. But time is wasting and a new road stretches before me. I'm leaving a hard-fought and hard-won career to become a bioarchaeologist. What does archaeology have to do with firefighting? Not a damn thing.

It's a cold clear morning in January and I've been up most of the night. The sky is still dark but there are fingers of daylight creeping over the eastern horizon. All that I own is crammed into boxes loaded onto a truck that sits quietly street side, awaiting the three-hour drive that will take me from the urban sprawl of Orlando to the shady hills of Tallahassee. In one week, I will enter the graduate program in anthropology at Florida State University. Today marks the beginning of a journey, one that will lead me to the excavation, analysis, and interpretation of human remains.

The days of heavy gear and chaotic emergency scenes are behind me: the weight of an air pack on my shoulders, the acrid smell of burnt synthetics in my nose, the pounding heat of fire as it consumes the room around me. These experiences slide into my memory, filed away with the drama and tragedy I've witnessed over the last decade. I want nothing more to do with pain. No more blood, no more cries for help, no more looking into the eyes of parents who have just lost a child. I want a clean slate, where I can explore life as it was lived thousands of years in the past through the bones left behind.

I walk out onto my balcony perched high above the city. It overlooks a small lake and the early morning sky is reflected in pale shades of copper. I look down on the truck that holds all my earthly possessions, a pale rectangle against the dark street. This is the last time I will stand here and watch the sky inch toward daylight. I've spent my entire career in this apartment, watching the seasons change: the sun sailing south with the approach of winter, then sliding north as spring arrives. I've seen countless full moons floating in the darkened sky, surrounded by faint stars that taper toward the horizon. My life has been here in these rooms, now stripped of all sign of me.

I shower and dress, packing the last of my things away for the short trip. By the end of the day, I will be settled in a new city with a singular goal: to make it through the next several years of grad school, tackling a Masters and PhD in Anthropology and learning everything there is to know about the human skeleton. Little do I know that this journey will take me well beyond Tallahassee.

I will travel to the gritty streets of London, the manicured lawns of Paris, and the rustic cities of Italy. I'll experience the tropical beauty of St. Croix, the vast landscapes of Ukraine, and the medieval countryside of northern England. I will work within the extensive collections of one of the world's best museums and experience the horrific drama of a forensics lab. I'll travel to these places with a primary purpose: to work on the bones of individuals long dead. I'll apply my experience of dealing with the sick and injured to those of the past, examining how they lived and how they died. I'm on my way to becoming a bioarchaeologist.

It's time to go.

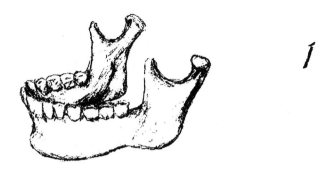

Laying the Groundwork

The city of Tallahassee is about as uncharacteristic a Florida city as you can find: a tree-filled landscape underlain by ancient red clay washed down from the Appalachian Mountains. Over twenty million years ago, Florida was a shallow, submerged limestone shelf, inundated by the Gulf Trough that flowed northeast over its surface. Millions of small marine creatures left behind their miniscule shells, forming the limestone peninsula that emerged from the seas as sediment from mountains to the north accumulated on the peninsula's surface. If you travel from north to south, your journey will take you through dramatic shifts in topography: from rolling clay to flat sand in a matter of hours.

Tallahassee was established in 1825, the result of a decision by the legislature to locate the capital between the bustling city of St. Augustine and the (still to this day) sleepy city of Pensacola. The name was bestowed by the Apalachee Indians who inhabited the area long before the Spanish arrived with their dreams of gold and religious conversion. In 1633, the Spanish established a chain of missions that stretched from St. Augustine to Tallahassee. Relying on the aboriginals' corn and generosity, the missions, along with the roads connecting them, were built on the backs of natives. Neither the missions nor the natives lasted long. By 1704, the missions were destroyed by British forces allied with the Creek and the remainder of the Apalachee fled the area. In 1763, it became a British possession, only to be ceded back to Spain twenty years later.

In 1818, General Andrew Jackson, no friend to the native, invaded Florida, driving the Seminole (not native to Florida but who were escaping from removal acts further north) into south Florida, where they still reside today. A year later, Spain relinquished control of Florida once again, this time to the United States. In 1845, Florida became the twenty seventh state. The state's thousands of documented archaeological sites tell the story of over ten thousand years of human habitation.

Anthropologists divide human history into cultural periods in order to provide a frame of reference for events in the past. These periods go by various names, depending on where you are in the world. In Europe, the terms Paleolithic, Bronze, and Iron Age define the region's history based on the types of artifacts produced at the time. In North America, using Florida as an example, these cultural periods are labeled Paleoindian (dating from around 12,000 - 9,000 BP; BP meaning "before present"); Archaic (9,000 – 3,000 BP); Woodland (also known as Transitional, around 3,000 – 1,000 BP); and finally the Mississippian, or Transitional (from 1,000 BP - European contact). Each of these periods is defined by cultural innovations that arose within their time frames.

Paleoindian peoples consisted of small, mobile hunter/gatherer populations that moved from place to place depending upon the availability of resources. The first people to reach Florida, their small numbers left scant evidence. Originally big game hunters, they shifted to smaller game as the megafauna vanished. Giant ground sloth, camel, mammoth, and saber toothed cats once roamed Florida's arid landscape, a landscape more similar to the great plains of Africa than the humid, tropical scenery of today. Through hunting and shifts in climate, these great beasts disappeared, to be replaced by the fauna of today – deer, black bear, panther, raccoon, and armadillo. The reduction in size of game was reflected in the reduction in size of the stone points used to kill them, which took place over ten thousand years ago.

The Archaic period ushered in many cultural innovations. Populations became larger, which required a shift to semi-permanent settlements; pottery was introduced in the region; the first shell mounds were deposited as people shifted to marine resources; regional stylistic differences in artifacts first appeared, and, most important of all (at least to a bioarchaeologist), the first formal cemeteries appeared on the landscape. The faint footprint of the Paleoindians was slowly replaced by a more visible imprint of human culture in Florida.

The Woodland period saw a continued increase in population densities, the establishment of permanent settlements, an increase in regional differentiation, and the introduction of earthen mound complexes. Pottery styles become more elaborate; trade networks increased as goods were exchanged over greater distances; and culture became more stratified, with a greater differentiation between commoners and elites. This social stratification is reflected in their burials, with some graves containing elaborate adornments of shell and ceremonial vessels, others containing nothing at all: archaeological evidence for the "haves" and "have nots."

The final period, the Mississippian, continued many of the traditions of the Woodland period, only on grander scales. Earthen mound complexes increased in size and number as social stratification intensified. Elaborate trade networks stretching from Florida to the Great Lakes brought metals to the region in exchange for the coast's beautiful shells. And agriculture took hold in northern regions of the state. Of course, all this changed with the arrival of the Spanish but that's another story.

Archaeology began in Florida, as it did in many areas of the world: as a form of antiquarianism carried out by curious residents and visitors. What lured the curious were thousands of shell mounds that lined the state's waterways and coasts. Primarily made up of clam, snail, or oyster shell, the mounds are the remnants of aboriginal cultures who subsisted on the rich bounty spilling from the numerous estuaries and pristine coasts among which they lived.

These mounds served a multitude of purposes. Some were merely refuse piles, known as "middens", remnants of generations' worth of meals consumed by aboriginal populations who occupied the area for thousands of years. Some mounds were intentionally built. Perhaps they began as middens but eventually served as valuable lookout points. Turtle Mound, located near present-day New Smyrna Beach on the east coast, once stood over seventy five feet high and, according to Spanish accounts, served as a launching point for the dugout canoes of the Timucuan Indians. It later became a familiar landmark for European ships entering the area, since the mound's sun-bleached shells could be seen for miles off shore.

Some mounds served as platforms on which the elite would reside. Many of these platforms were burned following the deaths of their rulers. These burned-out structures were then covered with more shell and the pattern would repeat. Excavations into many of these mounds reveal a layer cake of shell and burnt wood, with the occasional skeleton tucked in between.

The first novice excavations took place in the 1800s. Florida at this time was being transformed from a mosquito-infested backwater to a territory recognized for its rich natural resources; all of it just waiting to be exploited. The population was booming. Between 1840 and 1860, it went from a sleepy 54,000 to 140,000. By 1880, it reached 270,000, and Florida was on its way to becoming a prime destination for men of industry. Beginning in the early 1800s, citrus was but one of many exports shipped to regions far and wide across the county. Sugar and cattle soon joined the ranks, along with shipments of bear, deer, and panther hides. Although many resources were being sent out, the state's largest industry would become imports in the form of tourists escaping the ice and snow of northern winters. These tourists, many of them affluent, educated, and with means to travel, found a perfect diversion from the sun and sand by taking shovels to the many shell mounds of the region. What better way to spend an afternoon than by digging into the heart of a mound, recovering fragments of ancient pottery, beautifully crafted stone points, and the occasional human skull?

These avocational (and highly destructive) digs were later superseded by professional excavations. The Pepper-Hearst Expedition to Key Marco in 1896 was one of the first professional field projects conducted by trained archaeologists. They recovered beautifully preserved wooden artifacts produced by the Calusa Indians, who inhabited the area until the Spanish entered the scene, eventually conquering them and shipping the few survivors to Cuba. But the most notorious and well-traveled archaeologist was C.B. Moore.

Moore, the son of wealthy Philadelphians, was a curious sort with a deep interest in past cultures. He began wintering in Florida in the late 1800s, targeting the state's proliferation of shell mounds. Moore quickly realized that the majority of the mounds were inaccessibly located along the vast waterways of the state's interior, an area still lacking adequate roads. So he solved the problem by employing a fleet of small steamboats (the most famous, the *Gopher*) that afforded access to these remote treasures.

Moore's impact on Florida's shell mounds was a double-edged sword. As he had no formal training as an archaeologist, his excavations were highly destructive. Moore, however, took careful field notes, documenting the provenience of objects and skeletons recovered from the mounds and carefully conserving the artifacts he excavated. His field data serve as valuable records of his excavations and are still used today by students and professionals. The majority of the mounds he explored have since been destroyed, many of them mined for their shell, which was used to pave the early roads that crisscrossed the state.

Large-scale archaeological projects began with the Civil Works Administration, part of President Roosevelt's attempt to quell the economic devastation of the Depression. Florida archaeology provided a perfect solution: field work required a robust labor force, which meant jobs for the masses, and Florida's sub-tropical climate allowed projects to be run year-round. These projects, nine in all, spanned seven years and employed thousands of workers. They not only provided much-needed jobs, but also served as a foundation on which subsequent archaeological investigations would be built.

The Florida Park Service, established in 1946, played a fundamental role in the development of archaeology as a discipline and profession within the state. Its first director, John Griffin, began investigating sites throughout the state, recording their information in a site file he established at his office in Sebring, Florida. He and his staff were later moved to the Florida State Museum at the University of Florida campus, and they later sponsored the state's first archaeological conference, held in 1947 at Daytona Beach. The Park Service served as a major impetus for the establishment of archaeological programs at the University of Florida and Florida State University.

Florida State University's campus is a strange combination of history and modernity: beautiful, Gothic Revival buildings are flanked by the more modern (and much less attractive) red brick of the mid 1900s. The campus itself is landlocked within downtown Tallahassee, surrounded by the numerous administration buildings that house the state's government. In 1856, the city was designated as the site for a university based on its "salubrious climate" and its "intelligent, refined, and moral community."

Originally a boy's school, Florida State University became co-ed in 1858, when it absorbed the Tallahassee Female Academy. Known then as the West Florida Seminary, it began operation in 1857, just twelve years after Florida was granted statehood. It was renamed the Florida Military and Collegiate Institute in 1863 and produced young cadets who fought in Florida's Battle of Natural Bridge, one of the last confederate victories of the Civil War, making Tallahassee the only southern capital east of the Mississippi to avoid falling to the Union. In 1905, it reverted to a women's school called the Florida Female College. Finally, on May 15, 1947, the college returned to co-ed status and was renamed Florida State University.

Today, FSU is designated as a "Doctoral/Research University-Extensive" by the Carnegie Foundation. Formerly known as "Research 1 Universities," schools given this distinction are noted for their dedication to research, their commitment to awarding at least fifty doctoral degrees per year, and the securing of at least $40 million in federal grant monies. It also bears the honorable distinction of ranking among "America's Best Party Schools."

FSU's Department of Anthropology, which began with one archaeologist in the late 1940s, played an early role in establishing professional archaeology within the state. As archaeological investigations intensified, students and faculty from FSU and neighboring University of Florida in Gainesville conducted projects throughout the state. Data collection, research, and publications quickly established chronologies of early human occupation, naming and classifying stone points and pottery in order to identify temporal and spacial trends in artifact production, and establishing comparative collections that are still in use today.

I found anthropology by accident. Like many kids, I grew up a dinosaur freak, spending hours at a time staring at the books my mother provided me. I was enthralled by the landscapes, those cartoonish wetlands that show a myriad of dinosaurs, all browsing peacefully together while a distant volcano puffs on the horizon. Back then, dinosaurs were thought to be lumbering, cold-blooded giants, forced to spend the majority of their time wading through water in order to alleviate the tremendous stresses gravity placed on their gargantuan frames. The modern interpretations of dinosaurs are much different. Today, many of them are seen as agile, intuitive hunters and the issue of cold-bloodedness is still under debate.

Many people confuse the study of dinosaurs (paleontology) with archaeology (the study of humans through the material remains they leave behind). The confusion lies in the fact that both disciplines involve digging for evidence. But archaeology is a sub-field of anthropology and provides a means of examining humans via the "stuff" they leave behind. Pottery, tools, weapons, and especially skeletons – all of these serve as evidence of past lives and past practices that can be interpreted to understand ancient civilizations.

I had never heard of anthropology before discovering that the University of Central Florida offered a degree in the field. I had always been fascinated by human culture, as a result of my growing up a military brat who moved from place to place every two to three years. When I was a small child, my family was stationed in the Philippine Islands. I remember the mystery of the place – the people, their language, and the exotic foods they ate. All of it left me wondering about the differences in how we are raised, the customs we participate in, the values and traditions that encapsulate and define our lives.

Since my mother was juggling four small children, my father employed a live-in housekeeper, Mara. She was a warm, dark-skinned woman with jet-black hair flowing down her back. She would wrap it in elaborate twists and turns, an architectural mystery to me with my blonde pixie cut. She took care of our family, looking after four scrambling children and the menagerie of animals that shared our metal-roofed Quonset hut, standard residence for officers and their families. I remember the hammering on the roof and the rich smell of rain as we braced against the typhoons that regularly swept the islands, and I remember the feel of the ground swaying under my feet from the earthquakes that frequent the Pacific.

The Philippines were my first experience in a foreign culture, the basis for my interest in anthropology. They also formed the basis of my interest in medicine; it was a three-year stretch of the most accident-prone years of my life. My fascination actually began before the injuries. We would travel to the military hospital for our mandatory vaccinations for overseas travel, and I would thrill at the sights and smells of those sterile halls. The smell of rubbing alcohol, to this day, takes me right back. It was a place of

My father and I in Newport, Rhode Island, around 1966.

Our family home in the Philippines.

drama, with doctors and nurses rushing from room to room, attending the patients strewn within hallways and exam rooms. I would imagine the tragedies that had brought them to the hospital: attacks by wild animals, falls from multi-storied buildings, an array of emergencies conjured up in my immature imagination.

My introduction to trauma began when I fell from a picnic table. A girlfriend and I had been standing on top of the table when I lost my footing and landed on my back with my right arm twisted beneath me. I can still remember the loud "snap!" as the bones of my lower arm broke in two. My mother drove me to the hospital as I whimpered in pain, cradling my damaged arm in my lap.

I experienced my second injury on my father's bike. I was riding on the back of it one evening as he towed me through the neighborhood. Lost in the scenery, I forgot to keep my legs extended and my right foot went into the rear spokes, tearing the flesh from the top of my foot. This time I got to ride to the hospital in a police car, which was quite a thrill.

In the Philippines, during my accident-prone years with right hand and foot bandaged from accidents.

The third incident almost robbed me of my right eye. I was carrying one of our enormous cats through the house when I stumbled and fell forward onto a brass statue of a rooster. Its pointed feathers gouged my face between nose and eye. The doctor said that had it been a few millimeters to the right, the eye would have been history.

My most serious accident occurred when I happened to be sitting in a small, wooden camping chair, the kind that has scissor hinges that enable it to be folded flat. I had my right hand beneath one of the hinges when it collapsed, scissoring off the end of my right middle finger. Another trip to the hospital was followed by another scar on my small body.

My final injury occurred on Thanksgiving morning, when I decided to go outside and climb one of the many trees in our backyard. I was swinging from one of the branches, trying to get as high as possible when my hands slipped from the branch and I plummeted face-first onto the ground. I can still remember the taste of dirt and blood in my mouth as I realized I had knocked out both my front teeth. I spent the remainder of the holiday with a cold rag in my mouth, drowning in self-pity at missing the beautiful, golden turkey my mother had prepared. She believed at this rate I would never make it into my teens. I came away from these experiences with a fascination with trauma and a deep respect for medicine.

The three years I spent in the Philippines set the stage for my interest in the vastness of the planet and the range of people residing on it. I would walk to school and stare out over the airfields rimmed by purple mountains that glimmered in the morning sun. Although the islands are tropical, I don't remember the heat. What I remember are the smell of roasting pig floating across the metal fences separating the base from the poverty-stricken neighborhoods that rimmed its borders; the dirt between my fingers as my sisters and I hunted for small, pale gecko eggs hidden among the banana trees that surrounded our house; and the black bodies of bats that arrived each evening, blanketing the sky like dark moths. It was a magical place that awakened my interest in the world around me.

But I didn't know there was actually a field of study devoted to such interests. I sailed mindlessly through my first years of college, not knowing what I really wanted to do with my future. I figured as long as I stayed in school, I would eventually stumble upon something that would captivate me and propel me toward a four-year degree. That's when I discovered anthropology, sitting on the floor of my bedroom, thumbing through the course catalog for the University of Central Florida, reading through the various degree programs that filled its pages. When my finger ran across the word "anthropology", I paused, read the course descriptions, and knew I had found my calling.

I began classes in the fall of 1985. The classes were fascinating and I loved the atmosphere on campus, where I was surrounded by fellow students who shared my interest in learning and education. But the more I learned about anthropology, the more I realized that I had a long road ahead. I found that a bachelor's degree wouldn't get me anywhere; that if I was serious about the field, I would have to pursue at least a master's degree, if not a PhD. To a twenty one-year-old, that seemed like an eternity, an endless course of study. My restlessness won out and I knew I had to find a field of study in which I could get educated and get out. I wanted to be on my own, supporting myself, independent of my parents. So one rainy afternoon, I headed for the campus library to peruse the "careers" section. I found a large book of career paths and plunked myself down on the floor between the aisles and started searching. One job that had always interested me was that of a paramedic.

I grew up watching the show *Emergency* and always considered it an exciting and necessary field. What better way to help people than during an emergency, when they needed assistance the most? My father had always said that if you have a job in which you help people, you will always have a reason to get up in the morning. So I decided on the spot to pursue a new course of study: I would become a paramedic.

Well, becoming a paramedic led me to the field of firefighting, which led to a position with one of the finest departments in the state of Florida, the Orlando Fire Department. And now, fifteen years later, I'm back to anthropology, following an incredible career that, ironically, has made it possible for me to give up all I have worked for and head toward a career as an archaeologist. Life is strange and wonderful.

I settle into my new home in Tallahassee, a small apartment with a balcony that overlooks an eastern tree line. Classes begin next week, leaving little time to indulge in the homesickness I feel when I think of my previous life in Orlando. I focus on the tasks at hand: getting settled, learning my way around the city, and finding the campus bookstore so that I can purchase my books and get a jump on what I know will be a horrendous work load.

Human Osteology, the course that will be my introduction to the human skeleton, will not be offered until the fall semester, so I'll be taking three courses in the meantime—Geoarchaeology, Paleonutrition, and Seminar in Physical Anthropology. Geoarchaeology examines the physical processes of archaeological site formation, such as soil and sedimentation deposition, and how these processes affect the archaeological record. Paleonutrition focuses on faunal remains in the archaeological record. The remains from animals can indicate what people in the past were eating as well as their utilitarian use of animals and animal parts, such as hides for clothing or bone for tools. The Seminar in Physical Anthropology is one of four "core courses" required for the degree; the other cores are Linguistics (the study of the origin, spread, and relatedness of languages), Cultural Anthropology (the evolution and diversity of culture), and Archaeology (the methods and theory of archaeological excavation). Florida State's Department of Anthropology promotes this "four-field" approach to the "study of man," an approach that epitomizes American anthropology.

Classes are underway and the workload is intense. The Seminar in Physical Anthropology is a discussion-based course that integrates an endless number of journal articles on the biological study of human beings, which we debate and discuss during long, three-hour class sessions. Physical Anthropology, today more commonly called Biological Anthropology, comprises numerous sub-specialties. They include paleo-anthropology (the study of human evolution); primatology (the study of our primate relatives); forensic anthropology (the identification and analysis of human skeletons from contemporary contexts such as missing persons, murder, genocide, and mass disasters); bioarchaeology (the analysis of human remains from archaeological contexts); and paleopathology (the study of ancient disease). With my medical background, I naturally gravitate toward bioarchaeology and paleopathology.

I find Paleonutrition, commonly known as Zooarchaeology, incredibly challenging. The course objective is to be able to identify a myriad of animals from their skeletal remains. To do this, we must learn to identify individual species based on differences in their skeletal anatomy. I will learn the same technique with human remains when I take Human Osteology in the fall. Paleonutrition will also enable me to discern animal bones from those of humans, since this is the first order of business whenever remains are encountered in archaeological or forensic contexts.

We discuss the various types of archaeological evidence indicative of subsistence practices and environments based on the species of animals recovered from sites. Faunal remains also provide information about the life histories of the animals themselves. If you cut a cross section of an oyster shell, you can actually count the rings that have accumulated over the oyster's lifetime, giving you the age of the oyster at the time it was harvested, the season in which it was harvested, and its rate of growth throughout its short life.

Faunal remains also tell us much about the material culture of past peoples. The types of tools they made, the animals they utilized, and the breadth of weapons they produced indicate subsistence and cultural practices relied on by ancient peoples. Fishing barbs made of bone indicate reliance on marine resources; the reduction in stone points that accompanied the demise of megafauna, such as mammoth and giant sloth, indicates the shift to smaller game, such as deer and bear. We can literally read the past through the artifacts left behind. This is why archaeology is such a fascinating field. It speaks to our need to understand how people survived prior to modern conveniences, how they carved out a living in the wilds of early Florida.

Our exams consist of tables laden with the bones of numerous animals and fish, all requiring identification based on their shape (morphology) and type. The first order of business in determining the type and species of animal you are dealing with is to determine its general size. If the bones are small, are they from a small animal or are they the juvenile remains of something larger? The maturity of the bone is determined by the presence or absence of fused epiphyses, the ends of bones that permanently join the shaft when growing has ceased.

Skulls are a wonderful means of identifying animals. The size of the skull determines the overall size of the animal and the teeth are indicative of the animal's diet. The small, spiky teeth of the opossum are designed for crunching insects; the sharp canines of a bobcat for tearing flesh. The multi-purpose teeth of omnivores, like our own, can handle just about anything. Characteristics of bone also provide clues. The bones of birds are lightweight and hollow, a necessity for flight. Among fish, identification is based on the bones of their spines and jaws, which vary among species.

To prepare for our exams we use the comparative collections within our lab. The lab contains numerous species, primarily from the southeast;

they are typically encountered within Florida's archaeological record. For our term project, we are each provided an assemblage of faunal remains from a hypothetical archaeological site. Our task is to identify and quantify the various species within the assemblage in order to determine the types of animals being utilized at our "site." For this, the limited collection within our department is insufficient. We need a professional comparative collection, so we head for the Florida Museum of Natural History.

Located on the campus of the University of Florida in Gainesville, the museum, which was founded in 1891 as the Florida State Museum, began with the private collection of Frank Pickel. A professor of natural science at Lake City's Florida Agriculture College, he had amassed a collection of fossils and minerals that he used as teaching aids within his courses. As word of his collection spread, other professors donated their own objects and the collection grew until 1905, when the college was abolished. The museum was relocated to the new University of Florida in 1906. The collections were placed on temporary display in Thomas Hall (one of the halls along with Sledd and Fletcher that form a "UF" shape visible from the air) before finally being relocated to their permanent home in the basement of Flint Hall.

The museum's collections consist of archaeological, paleontological, ethnographic, and natural history specimens, accompanied by experts in each field. Their Florida Archaeology Collection includes artifacts from over 1,500 Florida sites spanning 12,000 years of human history in the state. The collection includes the artifacts and excavation records of some of Florida's first archaeologists, notably John Goggin, Ripley Bullen, and William Sears. These items are available for students and professionals alike and continue to serve as valuable references of the state's earliest archaeological endeavors.

The museum's Natural History Collections include Ichthyology (Fishes), Mammology (Mammals), Ornithology (Birds), and Herpetology (Reptiles and Amphibians), among others, along with a Genetic Resource Repository containing over ten thousand cryogenic (frozen) samples obtained from the Museum's vast collections, to be used in future genetic evolutionary and conservation studies.

The collections in the basement of Flint Hall are divided by category. We meet with faunal experts who assist us in identifying the fragmented remains within our samples. We spend the day poring over the bits and pieces of fish, reptiles, amphibians, birds, and mammals until we have each produced a long list of species which will serve as our final site inventory.

My course in Geoarchaeology examines how archaeological sites are impacted by the geological processes that surround them. Shifting landscapes, migrating rivers, and cataclysmic processes such as volcanic eruptions and earthquakes can affect a site's location, stratigraphy, and composition, making its interpretation problematic. An archaeologist's ability to "read the soil" encompassing a site enables her to determine whether or not a site has been disturbed since its deposition. This becomes critical when interpreting the site and even more important in the case of human burials. An archaeologist must be able to determine whether a burial is part of an archaeological assemblage or is "intrusive"; a burial dug into an existing site at a later time.

The Florida Geological Survey is a government institution that specializes in geoscientific research throughout the state. They conduct environmental assessments, collect data, and perform laboratory analyses that address issues such as water cleanliness and soil contamination. They are part of the Florida Department of Environmental Protection, and their offices are housed on FSU's campus. I've been given an incredible opportunity. I've been invited to accompany their geologists as they go below a large lake that recently and suddenly drained. I can't wait.

Lake Jackson is a large prairie lake that straddles the Red Hills Region of north Tallahassee. The lake is over seven miles long and covers about six square miles. On September 15, 1999, the lake disappeared. It literally drained away, leaving the waterfront homes on its rim facing barren grassland littered with dead fish. In the central portion of the lake, a large, eight-foot diameter sinkhole known as Porter Hole is one of many that drain the lake approximately every twenty five years. When the lake disappears, geologists take advantage of the opportunity to study the lake's underlying geology and its connection to the vast Florida aquifer that flows beneath the ground, supplying the majority of drinking water for the state.

I met Harley, one of the geologists, when he was a guest lecturer for our Geoarchaeology class. We became friends, spending time cruising across the dry lakebed, discussing the geology of the area and musing over the reaction of Native Americans who inevitably witnessed the same event over thousands of years. Lake Jackson is the site of an extensive earthen mound complex that sits on the south rim of the lake. Built by the Apalachee Indians around AD 1200, the largest mound rises thirty six feet. It produced beautiful artifacts during excavations in the mid-1900s. Burials recovered from the central portion of the mound were adorned with necklaces, bracelets, and one elaborate copper breastplate, accoutrements marking the elevated status of those interred and the extensive trade networks connecting the Apalachee to populations throughout the southeast and beyond.

I will have the opportunity to crawl into the belly of the lake, to see what a sinkhole looks like from within.

We assemble at the site just as the sun is rising over the eastern edge of the lake. It is late spring and the cool morning is quickly giving way to a

Ladders descending into the Lake Jackson sink. Photo courtesy the Florida Geological Society.

blazing hot day. Much of the equipment is already in place, since scientists have been working at the sink for several weeks. It's vital they wrap up their investigations before the summer rains ensue and flood the hole. We approach the sink, which resembles a muddy navel connecting the basin of the lake to the earth below. A narrow ladder protrudes from its center, one of several that provide access deep into the ground. The hole smells of rotting flesh from animals that have stumbled into the hole and died. We pass the large, putrid carcass of a turtle as we descend.

The first ladder rests on one of several plateaus within the hole. We climb down the first ladder and pivot to our left, trying to avoid the muddy sides that line the hole. We carry small lights that provide faint illumination in the ever-darkening pit. We descend a total of three ladders and find ourselves in a small cavern, about thirty feet below the surface. There is only enough room to squat and it can barely accommodate the two of us. Harley smiles and points to a small opening in the side of the cavern, just above our heads. It is low and dark, about the size of a fifteen-inch television. I take a deep breath of the fetid air as we head for the hole.

It's a tight squeeze, but the mud enables us to slither forward on our bellies. It's a strange sensation, being beneath the surface of the earth, knowing that millions of gallons of water have surged through this very hole, draining the vast lake in a matter of hours. The walls are a light brown and the mud is replaced by smooth rock. I run my hands along its surface, smooth and slimy as a fish's belly.

The air is cool, the smell of decay less pungent. I work the camera out of the pocket of my jeans, which are slathered in brown mud. I take several pictures, knowing I may never have another opportunity to photograph the interior of the earth. After a short break, we reverse our course, sliding feet first out of the small opening, into the small cavern and up the ladders toward daylight. We emerge filthy and tired but knowing we have glimpsed a side of the earth few will ever see.

As the semester draws to a close and I prepare for final exams and term papers, I'm planning my next semester. I've heard about a certificate program in Museum Studies that I can complete in conjunction with my degree. It will provide training in museum administration, collections management, and museum education, all of which will enhance my degree in anthropology since many of the largest skeletal collections reside in museums around the world. And since some of the best museums are found in Europe, that's exactly where I'm headed: to London.

I'll be taking two courses this summer: Museum Education and The History and Theory of Museums. The courses will consist of visits to London's numerous museums where we will meet with museum staff for a first-hand look at how some of the greatest museums in the world operate. I will share a flat with other students in my program in the heart of London, just down the street from the historic British Museum.

So now the planning begins. I need to obtain a passport and pack for a two-month stay. The course curriculum includes a trip to Paris for a short tour of their museums, as well. At the end of the semester, I'll head to Italy since I'll be in the neighborhood and have always wanted to see Florence and Rome. It's going to be one hell of a summer.

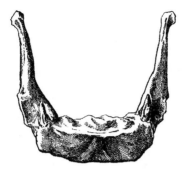

Going Abroad: London, Paris, Florence, and Rome

The sun is sinking in the western sky as the plane takes off, banking toward the northeast and heading for the dark Atlantic. We will fly along the east coast, skirting the rim of Canada and Greenland, and then making the short jump to Great Britain. We will fly in over Ireland and make our way to London by way of Wales.

Upon arrival, I meet up with a group of students, all converging on the city to pursue their own course of study. We gather our bags, inch our way through customs, then load onto a bus that will drop us in the heart of the city.

After an hour's drive, the bus pulls up in front of a white four-story structure, part of a row of buildings, all dating to the 1800s. We make our way into the lobby where a team of FSU administrators and their interns comb through clipboards searching for our names and room assignments. After reclaiming my bags, I make my way up three flights to what will be my home for the next two months.

We are in the heart of Bloomsbury, a fashionable neighborhood in central London composed of tree-lined streets and luxurious residences. Established during the seventeenth century, the area became the hub of hospitals and universities, its name synonymous with literature, art, and

The interior courtyard at the British Museum, the curved walls enclose the Library.

education. In 1739, the famed Foundling Hospital was established, housing abandoned children from the area in an effort to minimize the high rates of child mortality. The British Museum is one block to our east; the heart of downtown, including Trafalgar Square and the National Gallery, is a quick walk to our south. The famous theatre district spreads in several directions from our front door. Over the next two months, we will comb the majority of the city's museums, learning about their collections, their educational programs, and the role these museums have played in London's history.

There are over three hundred museums in London. Their collections range from art to antiquities to natural history. If you want to learn about museums—their history, scope, and purpose—there is no better place than London.

The word "museum" originates from the Latin *musaeum*, a place dedicated to the Muses, the nine mythical daughters of Memory who embodied intellectual and artistic achievement. The first museum dates back to the third century BC, the Museum of Alexandria in Egypt, which was actually a vast library where the learned went to pursue scholarly research. By the fifteenth century, as the Italian Renaissance was underway, collection of antiquities began as popes and royalty worked to reconstruct the history of the Roman world through their material culture.

As countries launched voyages of discovery around the world, they, like any of us today, wanted to bring back objects from their travels. One way of marking the extent of a country's reach was by collecting and displaying the "stuff" from their journeys. The collection of objects from different parts of the world also fueled scientific study. Explorers were commissioned to collect aspects of the natural world – plants, animals, and even people, so that scientists back home could examine, compare, and contrast this exotic booty.

In England, despite their extensive globe-trotting, museums didn't exist until the eighteenth century. Then Hans Sloane arrived on the scene.

The British Museum originally began in 1753 and today houses over thirteen million items representing human cultures from around the globe. The museum was established following an Act of Parliament on June 7, 1753, the result of bequeathal from Sir Hans Sloane to King George II. An avid collector and naturalist, Sloan accumulated over 71,000 objects in a personal collection he wanted safeguarded after his death. The collection consisted of plants, animals, coins, antiquities, and any other object that caught his fancy. Born in 1660 in Ireland, he arrived just as the "Age of Reason" was underway. This was an era of scientific exploration, during which people tried to gain a better understanding of the natural world by examining the fundamental principles of nature. Scientists wanted to understand nature without turning to the traditional biblical explanations they had relied on for centuries. Ships were sent abroad in search of new territory to investigate, sample, and settle.

A plant enthusiast, Sloan received his doctorate in physics in France, where he studied medicine and botany. In 1685 he returned to England, where he was made a fellow of the Royal Society. Founded the year he was born, the Society was a place for scientists to gather, discuss their research, and share information and ideas during their weekly meetings. Sloan became a fellow of the Royal College of Physicians in 1687 but it was in Jamaica where he spent fifteen months serving as the governor's physician, that he honed his skills in observing nature and collecting specimens. Jamaica is also where he was introduced to cocoa, which he had the foresight to mix with milk. He brought it back to England, where it was soon manufactured as a medicine and sold by local apothecaries. It wasn't until the nineteenth century that a family by the name of Cadbury began manufacturing chocolate based on Sloan's recipe, to be sold as a treat to the general public.

The British Museum opened on January 15, 1759, in what was then Montagu House, a sprawling mansion located where the museum stands today. The museum has grown over the centuries and, with the exception of both world wars, has been opened to the public since 1759. In December 2000, Her Majesty the Queen opened the controversial "Great Court", a steel and glass enclosure that encases the original courtyard between the sprawling wings of the museum. The resulting enclosure, spanning two acres, is now the largest covered public space in Europe.

Many of our days begin at the Museum. We target particular collections, noting the design of each exhibit and the messages that are imparted through the arrangement of objects and associated information. Objects in a museum are not randomly placed on display; each case is carefully designed based on the message intended, the context of the objects, and the aspect of culture the exhibit is intended to illuminate. Exhibits must take into account the cultures they represent, including their belief systems and customs. Sensitivity is mandatory when displaying objects from cultures whose values and traditions differ from Western perspectives.

In the United States, the Native American Graves Protection and Repatriation Act (NAGPRA) was enacted to address issues of cultural sensitivity toward Native Americans. Enacted in 1990, the act regulated the excavation of Native American remains on federal and tribal lands and also addressed issues of museum collections throughout the country which house human remains and ceremonial objects.

For hundreds of years, physical anthropology in America developed and grew based on the analyses of Native American skeletal remains. Scientists and "collectors"—those paid by scientists or scientific institutions—would pillage the graves of Native Americans, collecting specimens, especially skulls, to be measured and compared. In the 1800s, it was common for native groups to enter their cemeteries only to find their ancestors torn from the earth, a desecrated landscape left in the collectors' wake. The skeletons, along with the objects that accompanied them in the grave, lined the shelves of museums and universities throughout the country.

The beliefs and perspectives of their descendants were never considered. Finders' keepers.

NAGPRA put a stop to this, or at least forced the reevaluation of how museums and institutions treated the remains and ceremonial objects of Native Americans. With the implementation of NAGPRA, any museum or institution receiving federal funds must produce inventories of North American remains or ceremonial objects within its collections, including where the objects or skeletons were found, when they were found, and which tribal organization they were believed to be affiliated with. These inventories were then posted on the NAGPRA website. In consultation with federally recognized tribes, these "culturally affiliated" remains and objects were to be returned to the tribes to which they belonged, either to be overseen by the tribes or reburied, depending on the tribe's wishes and beliefs.

What has served as a form of redress for centuries of cultural insensitivity toward Native Americans has also forced institutions and the scientists that work within them to work with tribes to bridge the gap between respect for aboriginal belief systems and the need for scientists to learn about the history of the Americas, much of which depends on the analysis of human remains. In the best cases, both communities work together to achieve their respective goals. Scientists are afforded time to analyze the remains, collecting every ounce of information that can be obtained from the skeletons, which are then either returned to the tribes or kept in the collections where tribal members can actively participate in their curation. This "active participation" includes the tribe's ability to visit the remains, perform ceremonies, and insure their proper and respectful treatment.

As you can imagine, from a bioarchaeological perspective, the reburial of remains has potentially devastating consequences for the field. Once a skeleton is gone, analysis stops, the option of confirming previous studies is diminished, and there is no possibility for applying new analytical techniques as they are developed. Some of the field's most promising techniques, mainly molecular analyses, remain to be perfected, their potential for providing valuable information increasing each year as we learn more about these developing sciences. The reburial of remains removes the possibility of future research. Once a skeleton is gone, it's gone.

Our museum classes meet Monday through Thursday; the weekends are ours to do what we want. I spend my weekends mainly studying. I know I have another heavy schedule in the fall, and I'm trying to get a jump on my studies. My medical background (which includes courses in anatomy and physiology, biology, chemistry, and microbiology), will provide a substantial foundation for the analysis of human remains, which I will begin in the fall. So I spend most of my free time reading up on human anatomy and the changes in body shape and structure that accompanied our evolution. But when it comes to anatomical studies, London has quite an interesting history.

In the late 1700s, medicine as a professional discipline was just emerging in London. The first medical school (The Medical College based at the Royal London Hospital), opened its doors in 1785, producing some of England's first professional physicians, the most notable, John Hunter, a pioneer in early surgery.

During this "medical renaissance" there remained a singular issue impeding the training of young physicians: the number of students far exceeded the number of cadavers needed for dissection. Competition was fierce. Schools knew that the training of qualified physicians depended upon the availability of corpses; how was a young doctor to learn gross anatomy without experiencing it first hand? And how were young surgeons to be trained if they didn't understand the complex relationship, both structurally and physiologically, between internal organs? What was a body to do (sorry, couldn't resist the pun)?

The courts tried to rectify the situation by passing the Act for Better Preventing the Horrid Crime of Murder in 1752. Under the Act, anyone convicted of murder would suffer the punishment of dissection following a very public execution by hanging. The hangings were grand events. They took place at eight o'clock on Monday morning before large crowds – men, women, and children would gather before the gallows. Following the executions, the body would be left dangling from the gallows for one hour, a deterrent for anyone contemplating the act of murder.

But the law could not satisfy the need for bodies. In 1831, hundreds of anatomists were practicing yet only eleven bodies were available for dissection. Female bodies were an even greater problem. Between 1800 and 1832, only seven females were put to death. This dearth of female corpses meant that most physicians made it all the way through their medical training having never fully explored the female body. I'm sure it was even worse for the bachelors.

Medical students were struggling; medical schools were in "stiff" competition for corpses (again, I apologize). Then along came the "Burkers."

They say "necessity is the mother of invention"; so true. Enterprising individuals soon realized there was a fortune to be made in satisfying the medical schools' need for bodies and these men knew just were to go to find them. Let's imagine how it worked.

It is three in the morning and raining (it's usually raining in London) as two men dressed in dark clothing, shovels in hand, slink along the perimeter of one of the city's numerous cemeteries. The cemetery is not guarded; no fences or gates mar their way for what is there to protect among the dead? The men enter, making their way to the spot where earlier in the day they witnessed a string of mourners in silent procession. They locate the tell-tale mound of fresh earth, plunge their shovels into the soft loam, and quickly remove the overburden. The cheap pine box is no match for their tools. They dismantle the lid and lift the body from its dark hole, pocketing any valuables along the way. The body is stuffed into a large duffel bag and the trio quickly exits the cemetery. They cart the body through the dark streets, arriving at the back door of the local anatomy school where an "attendant" is waiting, cash in hand. The exchange is made and the next morning, a fresh corpse is waiting on the dissecting table as the young medical students file in for class.

This scene played out on a regular basis. Soon, cemetery plots evolved into small fortresses as families tried to keep their loved ones from being snatched. Iron fences, granite vaults, and layers of concrete dumped over caskets were some of the techniques employed to protect the dead. Further north, in Edinburgh, Scotland, things were even worse.

Two Williams, Burke and Hare, were Irish immigrants who arrived in Edinburgh in the early 1800s, looking for work. Their day jobs as laborers on the New Union Canal couldn't satisfy their financial needs, so they reinvented themselves as professional "resurrectionists." But breaking into cemeteries and digging up bodies required a lot of effort, especially after a long day of working on the canal. Burke soon devised a new scheme: why not simply pluck their prey from the streets of Edinburgh?

Who would miss the prostitutes that peddled their wares among back alleys and gloomy slums? Who would be concerned enough to report their absence? The technique of "Burking" was born.

Strangulation was the preferred method. The women were lured with alcohol and strangled as the opportunities arose. Strangulation was less destructive than other means of execution and resulted in a tidier corpse; no fuss, no muss. The victims were then delivered to local surgeon Robert Knox, who paid the bill and asked no questions.

When their murders reached into the double digits, Burke and Hare were eventually caught. Ironically, Hare agreed to testify against Burke, who was subsequently found guilty, hung, and dissected. His skeleton was put on display at the University Medical School; a purse made from his skin was gifted to the Police Museum. Both remain on display. Such is the story of early anatomical studies on the cheery island of Great Britain.

Our museum studies are not confined to London. We visit the beautiful towns of Cambridge and Oxford, which house several magnificent small museums on their campuses. Both universities are actually collections of colleges; Cambridge includes thirty one, Oxford, thirty eight. They began as one university, that of Oxford. But following a dispute among academics and townsfolk, a handful fled north and established Cambridge. They remain friendly rivals to this day.

The towns themselves are quite similar, although Cambridge lacks the charm of Oxford, both on and off campus. Cambridge's campuses are plainer, their lawns more structured and tailored. But the museums of both colleges are remarkable. In Cambridge, I visit the Sedgwick Museum, a small museum of geology and paleontology tucked within the college's campus. It's a slow day on campus and I am the only visitor in the museum. There is a quirky gentleman behind a counter; he smiles and strikes up a conversation. I explain to him I am an American student studying museums in London. He grins, beckoning me to the next room with a swift wave of his hand, and opens a draw that contains the most fascinating aspect of the museum's collections, objects collected from Charles Darwin's voyage on the *Beagle*.

The Sedgwick Museum of Earth Sciences, Cambridge, where many of Charles Darwin's collections are housed.

The five-year voyage, which he began in 1831, took him around the continent of South America and eventually around the world. He collected plants, animals, and rocks that would later provide him and generations of scientists samples from which to tease out the mechanisms of natural selection. It is astounding to look upon the rocks once held in his hands as he stood on the weather beaten coasts of South America, musing over the age and evolution of the earth.

We also take a day from our museum studies to play tourist—we are taking a day trip to visit Stonehenge and the city of Bath. We leave early in the morning on a small bus that makes several other stops at local hotels to pick up guests that will accompany us on our trip. We head out of the city as the noise from the morning rush fades in the distance. Like the Eiffel Tower in France, Stonehenge is one of England's most iconic structures. It originally began as an earthen work around five thousand years ago; the inner and outer rings of stone were later additions by Neolithic people living in the area. The large stones that compose the famous outer rings were transported from twenty miles north. Staring up at these immense stones, I'm baffled to think of the labor involved in their delivery.

As we approach Stonehenge, I look out over the vast rolling hills that surround it, stretching for miles in all directions. The sky is overcast, the clouds dark and heavy above the greens and yellows of the fields. It is very quiet. People speak in hushed tones as they approach the stones, as if entering a church. I make my way around the periphery of the monument. Where once you could touch the stones, the public is now held at bay by a roped barrier. This prevents the inevitable destruction of the stone by careless visitors wishing to bring home a piece of history.

We spend an hour walking about the site, imagining the people who built it, the people who lived around it and what it meant to their lives. Of all the places I have visited in England thus far, this is the most moving, the one I will remember always.

The elegant city of Bath is located almost one hundred miles southwest of London. The city was built by the Romans in AD 43. The majority of the city's buildings are made from pale local stone and the green hills provide a backdrop to the lavish homes that line the city streets. The focal points of the city are the hot springs that boil up from the ground. The Romans built elaborate structures surrounding the baths, and for thousands of years the springs served as natural spas for those seeking relaxation and the healing properties the waters were believed to possess. Today, you can walk the dim tunnels that connect the various springs within the building, picturing the Roman elite as they waded in and out of the warm murky waters.

As the day winds down, we gather at the bus for the long drive back to London. But we have one more trip to make before our semester comes to an end. We are off to Paris.

The train picks up speed as we head south out of London. The city fades in stages. The congestion and traffic diminish as the roads decrease in number; the beauty of central London gives way to the shabbier, crowded neighborhoods that rim its outer boundaries. Then, finally, we inhale the beauty of England's verdant landscapes as we make our way toward the southern coast.

The countryside takes on a rolling, liquid quality. The classic English hedgerows that give the country that puzzle-like appearance from the air

Stonehenge, on a surprisingly sunny day.

blur past my window as we head toward the darkness of the tunnel that will engulf us, and then spit us out onto the French countryside. I glimpse the blue of the English Channel as we descend into darkness.

The famous Roman baths with Bath Cathedral in the background.

We emerge in northern France, amidst small stone farmhouses dotting the landscape. The fields are markedly different from those of England. They lack England's manicured exactness, its tailored precision. The fields and farms of northern France are rustic and rambling. Even from the train, you get a feel for the ease and pace of life among the farms, a quiet simplicity that infuses the landscape.

The farms and fields give way to urban sprawl as we make our way into Paris. We will disembark from the train, board the underground and head to our hotel to check in. Two months of navigating London's Underground makes finding our way through Paris' labyrinthine subway system simple as we try to decipher the rapid-fire French streaming from loudspeakers throughout the station. What we don't realize until we arrive is that we are visiting during one of the city's most festive holidays: Bastille Day.

On July 14, 1789, the French Revolution kicked off with the storming of the Bastille, a prison that had symbolized the power of Louis the XVI's regime and its control over the people of France. The storming represented a fight against the oppression of its people, a symbol of liberty that marked the end of the monarchy and the beginning of France as a sovereign nation. It was declared a national holiday on July 6, 1880, and has been celebrated ever since.

The city is packed with soldiers representing armed forces from around the world. The soldiers will participate in a large parade that will wind through the city later this weekend. There will be much celebrating at the base of the Eiffel Tower, which is still adorned with thousands of white twinkle lights commemorating the millennial celebration of 1999. The city is a torrent of activity and we have much to see before the city is engulfed in festivities.

The first thing I notice as we make our way through the streets of Paris is the cleanliness of the city. I am used to the dirt and grit of London. The streets of Paris are swept clean, the sidewalks free of litter. The majority of the buildings are pale stone, giving the central part of the city a feel of clarity and lightness. Paris was transformed in the 1850s when Napoleon III hired civic planner Baron Georges-Eugene Haussmann. He developed a plan to restructure the city in order to ease the overcrowding that ham-

View from the top of the Eiffel Tower.

pered its growth and to minimize the epidemics that regularly carried off large numbers of its population. The project created new roads that enhanced traffic flow; established the grid and district system that today characterizes the city; built additional housing to ease the cramped conditions in which many lived; installed new sewers to funnel waste and runoff away from the city's center; and built public parks and monuments to enhance the city's overall appearance. Considered one of the greatest urban transformations in history, Haussmann's twenty-year project took a crowded, filthy, medieval metropolis and transformed it into one of the most elegant cities of the modern world.

Our whirlwind tour begins at Notre Dame Cathedral. Built in the twelfth century, the cathedral has served as backdrop for such notable historic events as the marriage of Mary, Queen of Scots in 1558; the coronation of Napoleon I in 1804; and the requiem mass for Charles de Gaulle in 1970. The next few days are a blur of activity as we attempt to take in a sampling of the many museums of Paris. Our first stop has to be the Louvre.

The Louvre began, not as a museum, but as a fortress constructed by King Philippe Auguste in 1190 to protect Paris from invading Anglo-Normans. Over the next several hundred years, it was transformed into royal residences and government offices, expanding in size and shape. Building after building were added, each designed to reflect the architectural styles of the day and the tastes of whoever happened to be ruling the country at the time. Within the royal residence, art collections amassed until finally, in 1793, the central part of the collection was opened to the public. By 1882, the collections had grown to such an extent that the royal residences were demolished and the modern Louvre was born, although the Finance Ministry continued to occupy one wing. Antiquities from around the world were added to the collections. By the early 1980s, President Mitterrand kicked off the Grand Louvre Project. The Finance Ministry was given the boot and the entirety of the structure was dedicated to art and antiquities.

The Louvre is a giant U-shaped structure with an open courtyard in its center. As we approach the huge courtyard, I am struck by the incongruity of glass pyramids perched within its confines, so out of place against the classic beauty of the museum itself. Erected in 1989 following the designs of architect I.M. Pei, the largest pyramid is surrounded by three smaller versions and provides an updated entrance to the museum. One actually enters the largest pyramid and descends down escalators to a subfloor that serves as the museum entrance, lined with numerous shops hidden beneath the courtyard. The original entrance could no longer handle the massive influx of daily visitors, so the new entrance was built to address this issue; the pyramids themselves are controversial artistic additions to the museum's grounds.

The public's reaction to the pyramids was mixed. Many criticized the addition of such modern pieces to such a classic landmark; others applauded the blending of modern and classic architecture. I appreciate both arguments. As you approach the museum, the pyramids are a shock, set as they are against the backdrop of the classic buildings that make up the museum. But the eye quickly adjusts and the pyramids transform into visual jeweled accents. They make for a dramatic entrance to one of the premier museums in the world, whether or not you appreciate their artistic nature.

We quickly realize we must target the objects we wish to see, since it would take weeks to stroll through the entire length of the museum's vast collections. We sit down with our guidebooks and highlight our areas of interest, then set a time and place to meet back. I head straight for the Mona Lisa.

When you approach the Mona Lisa, there is a dreamlike sensation to the event. First of all, the painting is much smaller than you would imagine; it appears almost diminutive against the extensive wall on which it hangs. I work my way through the large crowd gathered at her base to get a closer look at this magnificent work. I also take a moment to observe the crowd: the looks on their faces, the wonder in the eyes of those who have travelled, as I have, from countries far and wide to get a glimpse of this famous woman. It's amusing to see her wry smile set against the crowd as they stare upward, mouths agape. After several minutes, I make my way to other areas of the museum, trying to take in as much as possible; a difficult task in such an enormous place. By the end of the afternoon, we are drained from the experience, overwhelmed by the spectacular nature of the collections and awed by its size.

One of the most iconic symbols in the world, the Eiffel Tower is what I have been looking forward to the most. Although the museums of Paris are some of the best in the world, nothing says "Paris" like this amazing monument. Straddling an extensive green space that only enhances the beauty of the structure, the Tower is an intricately latticed work of iron named after the engineer who designed it, Gustave Eiffel. Built as the entrance arch to the 1889 World's Fair commemorating the centennial celebration of the French Revolution, it took three hundred workers over two years to assemble the Tower's 18,000 pieces of iron. The Tower was initially planned to be taken down when its twenty-year permit expired. However, over time numerous antennae were situated atop the structure, transforming it into a valuable communication tool and insuring its continued existence. Some of its notable visitors have included Thomas Edison and Adolph Hitler.

You can't appreciate the enormity of the structure until you stand directly under it. The breadth of its base reduces the people milling beneath it to miniscule proportions; ants under a picnic table. We make our way through the long line at the entrance, inching our way forward as we stare up in amazement at the ironwork shooting above our heads into the sky. It is dizzying to stare up through the central part of the Tower; your eye becomes lost in the maze of grid work that tapers to a point over one thousand feet up.

Once at the top, it is worth every bit of the waiting and shuffling in line. The view over Paris, all 360 degrees of it, is spectacular. You can truly appreciate the layout of the city, how the main thoroughfares spread like spokes of a wheel from the *Arc de Triomphe*; how the Seine glistens as it winds its way through the city. The beauty of Paris is magnified from this height.

I escape from the group the following day, hoping to visit *Le Catacombs*, Paris' extensive underground tunnels filled with skeletons. I've read about the tunnels and stared in amazement at the pictures of row upon row of human remains stacked neatly throughout its vast network. I arrive at the entrance to the sight, only to find it is closed for the month due to renovations. I wander back to the hotel, dejected and frustrated at the fact that I've come all this way and will miss out on what, to a skeletal nut, is one of the most fascinating attractions in Europe. Next time. . .

The next morning is dark and rainy. We find a small café televising the parade and watch in warmth and safety as we consume hot coffee and warm bread. The streets are flooded with brilliantly clad soldiers, the rain never diminishing their excitement at being part of the festivities. Exhausted after many days of exploring the city, visiting museums, and taking in the sites, we check out of our hotel and make our way through the Underground to the train that will whisk us through the Chunnel and back to England.

As the semester progresses, our museum visits become a blur. We see so many different museums, so many different exhibits, that our brains have become saturated. But I've made a wonderful contact at the Natural History Museum. I became especially interested in this museum because of its reputation as one of the preeminent natural history museums on earth.

The Natural History Museum in London is home to one of the largest natural history collections in the world. Housing over 70 million specimens, over 300 scientists, and an array of public education programs, the museum quickly became my favorite place in the city. It's hard to accurately describe. The beautiful buildings were designed by a young architect from Liverpool, Alfred Waterhouse, who was given the job when the original architect chosen for the project dropped dead. Waterhouse altered the original designs, producing the elaborate stone structure seen today.

The collections include every aspect of the natural world one can imagine. Over 55 million animals (28 million of which are insects), over 6 million plant specimens, and around 9 million fossils are carefully preserved in jars, boxes, and on shelves that form the bowels of the museum, the collections in which a cadre of scientists investigate the vexing issues of the natural world. And those are just the objects that were once alive. The collections include more than 500,000 rocks and minerals and over 3,000 meteorites that once rocketed through space. The museum also includes a library that houses the largest collection of natural history literature in the world. It is truly an astounding place.

My new contact is the Curator of Anthropology, Robert Kruszynski. He is a quirky, older gentleman who speaks in soft, staccato sentences, his hands fluttering erratically as he talks. I first contacted him via email when I was perusing the museum's website. He works within the Human

Origins Programme, a program within the museum's Paleontology Department, which houses a distinguished group of researchers that focus on the evolution of humans. The head of this program, Dr. Christopher Stringer, is one of the preeminent scholars on Neanderthals. His work has examined their evolution, their relationship to modern humans, as well as the exodus of modern humans out of Africa some 100,000 years ago. The Programme also houses a complete cast collection of all the fossils yet discovered representing the vast variety of species that link modern humans to our most ancient primate relatives.

Robert and I have been exchanging e-mails on a regular basis over several weeks. He sends me numerous articles on human origins and the analysis of ancient skeletal remains. After several weeks of correspondence, we meet for lunch at a small Polish restaurant tucked among the beautiful neighborhoods that surround the museum. There, we chat over exotic Polish fare, sipping vodka and exchanging stories about our lives. He lost many relatives during Hitler's ethnic cleansing programs; I'm fascinated and saddened to hear his stories of relatives who disappeared during his childhood. The conversation turns to science, and I ask him if there would be any way I could finagle a meeting with Dr. Stringer. I have read the majority of Stringer's books, and he is one of my favorite science authors. To have the chance to sit and discuss his work with him would be a thrill, a once-in-a-lifetime opportunity. Robert says he'll see what he can do.

I wait anxiously over the next few days, checking my e-mail obsessively for word from Robert. Finally, a brief note appears in my inbox: I am to have a ten – minute meeting with Dr. Stringer the following week.

The day of the meeting arrives, and I take the Underground to the museum, hoping the ever-present, curious aromas of the trains will not adhere to my clothes. I would prefer not to meet him smelling of curry and body odor. I sign in at the front desk and am quickly joined by Robert. I hurry after him as he ushers me into the dark, segregated halls of the Paleontology Department. He leads me among a maze of shelves containing the most fascinating specimens I have ever encountered. Giant skeletal heads peer down from above; humongous vertebrae stretch along endless shelves, winding like giant snakes in the dim light. I am thrilled to be among these incredible specimens, creatures that lived millions of years ago. I feel giddy by the time we arrive at Stringer's office, one of many that line the periphery of the collections.

Robert ushers me in and I stand nervously as a small, blond man quickly gets up from his desk, removing his glasses and offering a quick bow as Robert introduces us. We shake hands and I note the cool clamminess of his grasp. He sits me down, smiling in a shy and quiet manner. I express my appreciation for the meeting and am instantly put at ease by his kindness.

I pull out my list of questions, a bit embarrassed by the length and frenetic writing that covers several pages. But he sits patiently, endlessly smiling, and answers my questions one by one. Our ten—minute meeting stretches into an hour, then an hour and a half. As he is speaking, an idea flashes in my mind: part of my Museum Studies program requires a two—month internship at a museum. What if I can convince Dr. Stringer to let me return to the Natural History Museum next summer to intern within his program? As he is responding to my questions, my mind is racing with how to breach the subject. Knowing he has much more important work to attend to and that I have already blown my ten—minute allotment, I figure the worst he can do is turn me down and I will be no worse off. I have to take the chance. I know I will never have another opportunity so I decide to go for it.

We stand to shake hands once again. I quickly explain to him the provisions of the museum program and my need for an internship. "Would it be possible for me to return next summer to intern with your group?" I ask. I tell him I am willing to work in any capacity and would consider it an honor to work within their collections. He puts his chin in his hand, still smiling (which I take as a note of encouragement) and replies that although they have never had an intern before, he is certain they can find something to keep me busy. He tells me to have Robert make the arrangements; I'm ecstatic! Not only have I just spent over an hour with one of the top scientists in the field of human origins, but I've also gained assurance that I will be coming back next summer to work within one of the most distinguished research groups in the world. Dr. Stringer tells me he will assist me in any way he can.

As he walks me out of his office and we are rejoined by Robert, I can hardly contain my excitement. Dr. Stringer advises Robert to arrange the internship with one provision: he wants me to complete a course in human osteology before I report for the internship, so that I can work among their skeletal collections knowing how to handle and analyze human remains. I assure him that I will be taking Human Osteology in the fall and Advanced Osteology in the spring and that I'll be prepared by next summer to work on any project he is willing to give me. We shake hands a final time and I practically float through the department, thrilled to know my internship is secure and that it will be within such a prestigious institution as the National History Museum. I am also thrilled to have my return to London ensured. I thank Robert profusely and walk out of the museum, one step closer to becoming a specialist in the analysis of human remains, already thinking ahead to next summer. But before I head home, I have one more trip to take: I'm heading to Italy for some much-needed R & R!

I'm sitting in a small plane, staring down at the snow-capped peaks of the Italian Alps as I make my way to Florence, Italy. I've never been to Italy, I know little about its history, and I don't speak the language; this is going to be interesting.

The plane touches down as the late afternoon sun sinks toward the horizon. The air is stifling, still, and hazy; the small airport noisy and crowded. I've shipped my books and the majority of my clothes back to Florida, so I gather my bag and make my way to the taxi stand. Pointing to my hotel on the crinkled map I bought prior to leaving London, I smile, hoping the taxi driver will take pity on me and transport me in the right direction.

I'm dropped on a narrow street in front of a small hotel tucked within the tall buildings that line the street. I enter the lobby and begin a broken communication with the front desk attendant, who smiles broadly as she checks me in. She escorts me up to a small, stifling room and I instantly realize there's no air conditioner. I patiently explain to her that I booked an air conditioned room and will not settle for the small sauna in which we stand. After stopping in another small, hellish room, I smile and shake my head, indicating there is no way I am going to settle for this little hot-box on my first trip to Italy. Finally, she brings me to a lovely cool room overlooking the narrow street. I nod in agreement as a small air conditioner hums in the background. I have arrived.

I quickly unpack and head for the streets. Florence is a maze of narrow, winding, cobbled streets that merge and split at random. Most of them curve between ancient buildings that cast deep shadows on the city. My first stop is the Arno. Growing up a Navy brat, I am happiest when close to water. So I travel the few blocks until I am standing alongside the river, flanked by bustling shops and restaurants. The sinking sun has turned the entire city an orangey copper and I find it hard to believe I am here.

The city of Florence was first established as a permanent settlement two thousand years ago. Around 50 BC, Julius Caesar transformed it into a military garrison due to its strategic location along Rome's northern path of expansion. During the medieval period, around the twelfth century, Florence became a city-state but it was the emergence of the Renaissance that really put Florence on the map. Architecture, painting, writing, and philosophy blossomed within this small city, producing some of the world's most famous artists and works. By 1425, the population had grown to over sixty thousand and contained twelve artist guilds, powerful mem-

Sunset over the Arno River, Florence, Italy.

bers of the community organizations that controlled trade and commerce, making it one of the wealthiest cities in the world.

Even today, Florence is considered one of the art capitals of the world. Although the city covers less than forty square miles, it attracts millions of tourists who come each year to see what is considered one of the most beautiful cities on earth. In 1982, Florence was declared a UNESCO World Heritage Site based on its history, art, and architecture. You can spend entire days simply wandering the streets, admiring the beautiful buildings, and that's exactly what I intend to do.

I spend the remaining hours of daylight roaming the winding streets until I find an open piazza lined with crowded restaurants and street performers. I take a table outside and the elderly waiter brings me a carafe of sweet, sparkling wine that soothes my parched throat. The sky turns pale blue as the first stars appear and the bells from the Duomo cathedral chime in the distance.

The evening is dreamlike. I am removed from classwork, museum tours, and the oppressive companionship of my flat mates. To sit by myself and enjoy the sweet wine, knowing I have the next week to do as I like, infuses me with an incredible feeling of freedom. A large plate of steaming pasta laced with a delicate tomato sauce arrives, and I inhale the pungent smell of fresh herbs. I watch the people in the square, wondering where their journeys originated, where they will end. I love to watch people, especially while travelling. Culture is so regionally defined that, even within the States, you don't have to travel far to find varieties of dress, food, and social customs. Being in a foreign country is anthropological observation on steroids.

Nevertheless, having spent the last two months in London (where on any city street you encounter people from every corner of the world), I've become acclimated to a multicultural setting. I quickly slide into the pace and cadence of Italy.

The people of Florence are friendly, the atmosphere warm and inviting. You can't walk down the street or sit in a restaurant without being greeted and drawn into conversation. As I finish my meal, I am quickly adopted by a large family sitting close by. They speak no English but there is a young boy among them who knows a few words. The adults are drinking and laughing, motioning for me to join them. The boy welcomes me

The ornate exterior of the Duomo in Florence.

with broken English and the only information I can glean from him is that he likes computers. After a while of smiling and nodding, I thank them and graciously take my leave to join the crowd in the square as they gather around a small group of street performers who cajole the crowd to throw money into their hats.

I wander back to the river; its dark surface reflects the lights of the buildings that line its shore. The air is cool and a quarter moon climbs the evening sky. I slowly make my way back to the hotel, where I fall asleep to the noise of traffic below.

I spend the next few days wandering the city, visiting the colorful buildings of Florence. I round a corner and find myself in front of the Duomo, a monstrous Gothic structure. Its famous dome, engineered by Filippo Brunelleschi, protrudes high above the jagged roofs of the city and is a reminder of the birth of the Renaissance. Built at the end of the thirteenth century, and following the designs of Arnolfo di Cambio, the church took over 170 years to build. The rambling buildings are decorated with pale pink, white, and green marble, giving the entire structure the look of an elaborate wedding cake. The bells toll regularly and can be heard throughout the city. To stand under the dome inside the cathedral, and to look up into the beautifully designed pale frescoes that taper within its point, is to breathe in the history of the place.

The food of the city is wonderful. I've been surviving for the last two months on sandwiches and fresh fruit, since our kitchen in London was too small to keep large stores of food. So I indulge in the wonderful pastas, fresh breads, and plentiful vegetables found throughout Florence. Each meal is a joyous, carb-laden experience, and the hot afternoons are quenched by frequent stops at the gelato shops that dot each corner.

Florence, like London, contains world-famous museums, among them the Uffizi, which houses works by Rubens, Botticelli, and Michelangelo, among others; Pitti Palace, the Renaissance residence built in 1458 by the Florentine banker, Luca Pitti; and the Palazzo Vecchio, Florence's town hall that opens onto the bustling plaza of Signoria, where a copy of Michelangelo's statue of *David* stares out over bustling crowds. One of Florence's most famous artists is one of my favorites, mainly due to his beautiful drawings of the human skeleton: da Vinci.

Leonardo da Vinci was born on Aril 15, 1452, in the small village of Anchiano, Italy. The illegitimate son of a notary, he and his mother relocated to Florence with his father, who intended young Leonardo to follow in his footsteps. However, this plan was sidelined when Leonardo was introduced to Andrea del Verrocchio, who ran one of Florence's most successful artistic workshops. At the age of fourteen, Leonardo began an apprenticeship that would change his life. The work put him in contact with some of Italy's up-and-coming artists, and by 1472 he was working as a professional painter, bouncing back and forth between Florence and Milan.

Leonardo's interests weren't limited to painting. He had a gifted scientific mind and applied it to the fields of astronomy, zoology, geography, paleontology, and engineering. But it was the combination of his gift for painting and his keen interest in anatomy that led to some of his most exquisite drawings: those of the human body.

Da Vinci was introduced to anatomy during his apprenticeship. He knew that if the body proportions were incorrect, his renderings would be inaccurate, so he meticulously applied mathematical measurements to the skeletons and cadavers that served as his subjects, resulting in beautifully precise anatomical recreations. Much of his knowledge was obtained through the dissection of human cadavers. Dissections, illegal at the time, afforded him a glimpse inside the human body, where he explored how muscles attached to bone, how bones articulated, and how the internal organs were arranged.

Leonardo's drawings filled a gap in anatomical studies of the time. Most medical information was presented in written form, with few diagrams available for students of medicine. Da Vinci quickly realized that his art provided re-creations of the human body that could be used to navigate and better understand human anatomy. His illustrations of human embryos within the womb were the first ever created, although they were lost for centuries before being rediscovered in the twentieth century. His most famous anatomical work, *Vitruvian Man*, is a perfectly proportioned male set within a circle and square, accompanied by geometric descriptions based on the work of famed Roman architect, Vitruvius. Created around 1487, the work is a beautiful culmination of da Vinci's artistic and scientific expression.

Two days in Florence and it's time to head to Rome. I board the train mid-morning, having left the bulk of my belongings at the hotel where I will return in three days. As the train speeds through the countryside, I stare out over vast yellow fields that line the tracks. When the train slows, I realize the yellow is that of sunflowers, their giant heads bent toward the early sun.

I arrive in Rome and head to my hotel, a large, elegant establishment in the heart of downtown. All of Rome seems larger and grander than the quaint streets of Florence. A metropolitan side of Italy, Rome is a city of movement. The streets are wide thoroughfares where maniacal drivers speed in every direction. Interlaced among the cars are scads of scooters, their brave drivers darting in and out, oblivious to the danger that surrounds them. The sidewalks are jammed with people who move with a speed that mirrors the frenetic traffic. To stand on a street corner is to watch the city whirling past, a blur of color and commotion.

Rome has always been a place of action. Inhabited for over two thousand years, it evolved from kingdom to republic to empire, eventually being deemed the capital of the Kingdom of Italy in 1871, the capital of the Italian Republic in 1946. It has been the seat of the Papacy since the first century AD, housing the "Bishop of Rome" (commonly known as the Pope) and his small city-state, the Vatican.

I stop for my first sample of real Italian pizza, which is a cracker-like crust, topped with cheese, fresh herbs, and sliced tomatoes – simple, yet wonderfully flavorful. By late afternoon, I make my way through downtown when I happen to turn onto a side street. I suddenly look up and am face-to-face with the Colosseum. It takes my breath away.

Construction began in AD 72 under the ruler Vespasian, and took only eight years to complete. Built as a "pleasure palace for the people," this enormous structure could house over fifty thousand spectators and was based on sophisticated designs. The ruins that stand today are but a hint at the structure's original majesty, at one time adorned with gilded bronze shields and retractable awnings that could shade about a third of the spectators. It is too late in the day to visit—I will come back tomorrow to tour the interior. So I breathe in the night as a pale moon appears between the crumbling arches of its upper decks.

I wake late the next morning and head down to breakfast in a sun room overlooking the gardens in back of the hotel. The coffee is strong, the bread warm. I make my way out onto the street and am hit with the intense heat of late summer. The air is heavy and stifling, the mercury already rising into the thirties, which in Fahrenheit equates to "hotter than hell." I head straight for the Colosseum.

A long line winds its way around the base of the structure, as people wait patiently to get in. The crowd is entertained by men dressed as Roman soldiers who good-naturedy demand money to have their pictures taken with the tourists. Numerous stray cats wander among the crowds, no doubt fed by the tourists who flock to the site. The only thing outnumbering the cats are the nuns, who amble along, oblivious to the heat. I hope for their sake they are naked under their habits.

The Colosseum, which opened its doors in AD 80 under Emperor Titus, was the largest amphitheater ever built by Romans. It took only eight years to build and was originally called the Flavian Amphitheatre. It is most famous for the bloody contests fought among gladiators, captured slaves taken in battle or convicted criminals whose stage names were based on their fighting styles and choice of weapons within the arena. Swords, lassos, chariots, and spears were among the murderous weapons employed for the staged battles. Combatants were typically dressed to resemble barbarians and their battles depicted famous victories of the Roman Empire.

The games originally began in 264 BC and quickly became a popular public sport, eventually spreading throughout the Roman Empire. Their original purpose was to honor the death of elites who privately funded the games. Over time, as their popularity spread, funding of the games shifted to the state, which eventually funded schools where the gladiators were trained. The contests featured battles between men but also included battles against wild animals. Known as *bestiarii*, these games pitted man against a range of beasts, including leopards, lions, bears, and even elephants and the slaughter of animals could reach the hundreds during a full day of battle.

Archaeological excavations of gladiator burials from Roman-period York, England, reveal well-built males with numerous forms of traumatic injuries that were inflicted just prior to death. The burials date between

AD 70 and 410 and reveal the horrendous nature of this bloody sport. Blade injuries, hammer blows to the head, and decapitations are found among the dead.

Nuns strolling in front of the Coloseum, Rome.

To stand in the middle of the Colosseum is to imagine what must have gone through the minds of those made to fight within it. The battles typically ended in the death of one of the combatants, the crowd usually deciding the fate of the loser. These battles reduce our modern sports to inconsequential games in comparison. Elaborate tunnels ran underneath the entire structure, hallways funneling both men and beasts into the arena.

Today, the floor of the arena is covered in sawdust. The air is heavy with heat and dust and the smell of fresh cut wood drifts throughout the structure. The silent stone arches have witnessed thousands of deaths; they stand as sentries of the past, their crumbling exteriors the result of fire, earthquakes, and thieves who removed massive amounts of stone to use as building materials.

I spend the next day trying to escape the intense heat. It saps me of much of my ambition to site-see. Aside from the heat, my brain has been crammed with more information than it can possibly process. The sights, sounds, and experiences of all the places I've been in the past two months are overwhelming. London, Oxford, Cambridge, Paris, Florence, and now Rome; my head is a blur of activity and I'm exhausted. I simply want to relax and not think.

The Coloseum, Rome.

But I'm not too tired to see skeletons. I've read about the numerous catacombs that run beneath the grounds surrounding the city, so I take a bus to the outskirts of town, amidst rolling green hills and sun-baked fields. The catacombs were the result of two things: the need for space and the need for dirt. Christians of the time shunned cremation as a form of burial, since the body was kept in its earthly form to prepare for the day when it would rise from the grave. Thus, their burials required an earthly tomb. Knowing it was but a matter of time before there was no more space within the city's cemeteries, they chose the outskirts of town to dig vast tunnels where individuals could be laid to rest. Laws of the time forbade burial within the city's limits, so the catacombs were relegated to Rome's countryside.

Although the dark tunnels are a welcome relief from the afternoon's blazing heat, I'm astonished by the lack of bones. I wander through the maze of alcoves and stone altars where bodies once resided, but alas, not a bone in sight. I'm sorely disappointed. Although the tunnels are fascinating architecturally, I was hoping to see piles and piles of human remains, stacked in whimsical fashion like *Le Catacombs* of Paris. I'm let down as I emerge into the bright afternoon, my desire for bones unquenched.

I visit a few of the smaller museums, noting the vast differences in layout and design from those of London and Paris. The lack of air conditioning in some of them astounds me; I wonder how they manage to protect their collections from the intense heat and humidity. At night, I head down to Trevi Fountain, where crowds throng the steps surrounding it. The water that flows from the Fountain careens through a twelve-mile aqueduct system constructed in 19 BC, supplying the numerous fountains in the city's historic center. In the center of the fountain, Neptune, the god of the sea, is perched upon a chariot pulled by two sea horses. The fountain serves as an evening gathering point for the masses that flock downtown and is a hot spot for music and socializing. I watch the water cascade over the rocks, thinking of the journey it has taken to reach central Rome. I think of my own journey, from the encapsulated world of a firefighter to some of the grandest cities in Europe.

I return to Florence, where I spend the last of my European adventure walking the narrow streets and shopping the open-air markets. I take a cab to an overlook high above the city. From this vantage, I look out over

Crowds gathering in the evening at Trevi Fountain, Rome.

all of Florence as the sun burns out in the sky and the air begins to clear. I return to my hotel and head to the rooftop. I take a glass of wine and sit as a faded orange smear stains the horizon, my last night in Italy.

Tomorrow I will fly back to London and board a plane to the States. I will return to Tallahassee and prepare for school. There is much before me. The fall semester will begin shortly; the bulk of my education lies ahead.

My next semester will focus primarily on Human Osteology, where I will learn to identify every fossa, groove, and landmark of the human skeleton. This will be followed by a semester of Advanced Human Osteology, during which I will learn how to determine the sex, age, and height of an individual; assess traumatic injuries and identify pathological lesions exhibited among their remains; and tease from the bones every bit of information that will lead to a better understanding of the health of ancient populations.

I know the next two semesters will shape my professional future. I will apply the science and medical training of my past to focus on the health and disease of past peoples. I will contrast the traumatic injuries I treated on live patients during my tenure as a paramedic to those sustained by individuals living thousands of years ago. What I don't realize at the time is that housed within FSU's Department of Anthropology resides one of the most important skeletal populations in the world. I will spend the next ten years of my life investigating the health of this population, whose remains were excavated from a small pond in eastern Florida. I am about to meet the people from Windover.

3

Skeletons from the Pond

The city of Titusville is located on the east coast of Florida, about two hours south of Jacksonville. Founded in 1867 as the town of Sand Point, the city was later renamed after Confederate Colonel Henry Theodore Titus, who came to the area to establish a town on land owned by his wife, Mary. She and the Colonel established "The Titus House," the first hotel in the area, and donated tracts of land for the establishment of a courthouse and several churches. It would take a decisive domino match to determine the new name for the up-and-coming town. Captain Clark Rice, who envisioned the town of "Riceville," agreed to the game, but lost. The victorious Colonel slapped his name on the town, and it was renamed "Titusville" in 1873.

Like many cities along the east coast of Florida, Titusville is separated from the Atlantic Ocean by the vast Indian River Lagoon system. The Lagoon runs 156 miles along the coast and is the most biologically diverse estuary in North America. It is home to over 4,000 species of plants and animals that reside within the rich saltmarshes, seagrass meadows, and mangrove forests that make up this extensive system. With over 700 species of fish and 300-plus species of birds, the Lagoon has provided natural resources to people living along its shores for over 10,000 years.

In May 1982, construction was underway on a sprawling subdivision to be called Windover Farms. The subdivision, which is bordered by the

St. Johns River to its west and the Lagoon to its east, would consist of ranch-styled houses set on large plots of land and would eventually cover several square miles.

On this particular morning, the last cool traces of spring were giving way to the heavy heat of approaching summer. The first hints of summer storms that pound central Florida each afternoon were gathering on the horizon. A backhoe operator, working alongside a small pond, was clearing the edge of the pond to make way for one of the many roads that would wind through the complex. As his machine scraped the soft, blackened soils from the pond's edge, he happened to notice a shiny object among the spoil pile. He climbed down from the machine, taking a welcome break from the heat and noise, only to find that the shiny object blinking in the glaring sun was a human skull, staring back at him from the dark earth.

He was not about to get back on the backhoe. Instead, he immediately notified his foreman, who then notified the land owner, a conscientious developer who took an interest in the impact his projects made on surrounding landscapes. The developer notified law enforcement, who then notified archaeologist Glen Doran from Florida State University. When Dr. Doran arrived on scene, the first thing that struck him about the skull was the teeth.

They weren't like our teeth. Their surfaces were highly worn, the first hint at their antiquity. The soft, highly processed foods we consume today cause little wear on our teeth during life. But among prehistoric populations, it was a different story. A lifetime of ingesting grit mixed in with their food resulted in the wearing down of the teeth among many ancient populations. Picture yourself at a picnic on the beach. Inevitably, sand finds its way into your sandwich and before you know it, you feel the familiar crunch of sand mixed in with your tuna fish. Now magnify that into a lifetime of consumption. The grit of the sand works like fine sandpaper. It slowly erases the enamel until your teeth are half their original size, their surfaces flattened to a level plain. Those lucky enough to live into old age somehow survived with mere stubs.

Teeth were also used as tools. Who among us hasn't clamped down on our toothpaste cap in order to crank it open? In lieu of vice grips, ancient people tended to use their teeth as grasping tools; holding hides while they were scraped or sewn; softening leather by chewing it. When Doran noted the heavy wear patterns among the teeth, he knew they were dealing with a prehistoric person. He could never have imagined just how ancient this individual would turn out to be.

The developer was gracious enough to pay for radiocarbon dating of the skull and when the dates came back, they were astonished to find it was over seven thousand years old. What was even more astounding was that the individual had come from within the pond. This small pond would turn out to be one of the most important archaeological sites ever discovered. The site would be called Windover.

The most ancient human burials date back to the Middle Paleolithic (200,000 – 45,000 year BP) period, serving as the earliest evidence for ritualized behavior among *Homo sapiens* and Neanderthals. In some cases, bodies were stained with red ochre and placed in shallow graves, along with grave goods. Since then, burials have taken on numerous forms as cultures around the world express their belief systems, values, and customs in the ways they inter their dead. The majority of archaeological information comes from the examination of human burials; preparation of the body, its position in the ground,

The exceptionally preserved remains at Windover, pedestalled before they are removed. Photo courtesy G. Doran.

and the objects that accompany it all provide valuable information about the people performing the interments.

With a seven-thousand-year-old skull in hand, Doran knew they had stumbled upon a truly exceptional find. Most prehistoric burials in Florida have little chance of persisting within the archaeological record. The naturally acid, sandy soils of the region are highly destructive to skeletal remains. The soils basically dissolve the skeletons and archaeologists are lucky to recover a few bone fragments and teeth. But because the people of Windover were placing their dead within the pond, tucked in the anaerobic peat that happened to be of a neutral pH, their bones remained well-preserved for over seven thousand years and would hold numerous clues concerning life during Florida's Archaic period.

Florida's porous limestone geology and high water table result in the state being dotted with numerous small bodies of water. There are around 8,000 lakes, over 2,000 rivers, and approximately 350 named springs within in the state. By the beginning of the Archaic period, surface water and shorelines were close to what they are today; more surface water meant more prime spots for human settlement. Aboriginals chose locations adjacent to freshwater resources for their settlements to ensure adequate water supplies for drinking, utilitarian purposes, and obtaining food. But they also used these bodies of water for another purpose: they used the ponds and springs for burial of the dead.

A "mortuary pond" is the term used to describe burials using natural bodies of water; they are basically "pond cemeteries." Windover is one of five mortuary ponds that have been discovered in Florida, all of which date to Florida's Archaic Period (which began around 9,000 years ago and ended about 3,000 years ago).

These "mortuary ponds" are found only in Florida and only during the Archaic Period. At no other time and nowhere else in the world do we find this custom; it is unique to Florida's Archaic peoples. What started as a single skull in a spoil pile would turn out to be the largest mortuary pond ever discovered and one of the most significant archaeological sites in North America.

The Florida legislature provided funding for three years of archaeological fieldwork. At the end of three years, the remains of 168 individuals had been carefully excavated from the pond's base. Recovered from these intricate burials were artifacts, such as tools made from bone, wood, and antler; shells used for personal adornment; and, most astonishing of all, hand-woven textiles which were wrapped around many of the individuals in death. The grave goods have afforded a glimpse into life among ancient

Floridians: their customs, habits, and means of utilizing the natural world around them in order to survive in the challenging environments in which they lived.

But the skeletons weren't the only aspects of their bodies that survived in the pond. Their skulls, which protected their brains during life, also protected them in death. Over ninety of the crania contained remnants of the brain that once guided its owner through the rigors of life in ancient Florida. These tissues afforded one of the first glimpses of ancient DNA, tracing the people of Windover back to their Asian roots. How and when they arrived is still a mystery.

The plants recovered from the burials provide a wealth of information as well. Some of the skeletons contained small concentrations of seeds in their bellies, evidence of their last meal or perhaps attempts at end-of-life pain control, since many of these plants have known medicinal applications. Wild grape, nightshade, and elderberry, all natural sources of pain relief, were found within the abdominal regions of some. Other plants within the graves, such as the sticks erected over the bodies, indicate the pond was used during the late summer and early fall months; it was probably part of their annual migration route through the area. Where they were living is a mystery, as no evidence for living sites was recovered at the time of excavation.

Let's step back seven thousand years and observe a burial ceremony along the shores of Windover pond.

A small group gathers at the shore. The pond is rimmed by rugged flora native to the area. Pond willow, cattails, and dog fennel line its outskirts, while inland, cabbage palms and saw grass spread like an impenetrable blanket over the sandy soils. The area is shaded by the outstretched limbs of hickories and pines. The people huddle together in a solemn circle as a low mist glides along the mirrored surface of the pond and the smell of wood smoke permeates the air. They mourn quietly, each of them familiar with the grief of loss. This will be the final resting place for a young boy who will join the many who have gone before him.

His small body is placed in a semi-flexed position, his legs tucked up against his body, his arms folded alongside. His body is wrapped in matting made from the leaves of local palms. Tucked against his body are

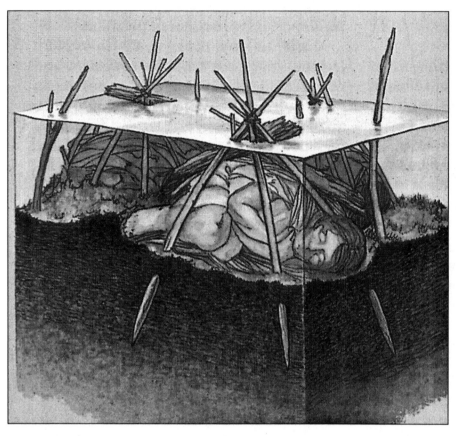

An artist's rendering of a burial at Windover showing individuals wrapped in woven matting. Photo courtesy G. Doran.

objects he used in life. Tools made of antler and bone, shells gathered from the coast. These objects are secured within the wrapping and the body is waded out into the pond. The small bundle is pushed below the surface into the dark peat at the pond's base. Once in place, a small erection of sticks are placed teepee-style over the body to anchor it to the pond's floor and protect it from predators. A single stick is driven into the muck near the body to mark its location. The mourners pay their last respects and filter back into camp as the surface settles over the grave and the sun disappears through the trees.

Why the people from Windover used a pond for the burial of their dead is unknown. Their well-preserved skeletons along with the objects that accompanied them to the grave have shed light on the material culture and practices of ancient peoples but we can only speculate as to their intention of ponds as cemeteries. As for their skeletons, the excellent preservation within the pond affords a glimpse at life, death, and injury among this ancient population. So how do we obtain this information? First, one must learn how to read the bones.

Windover pond today.

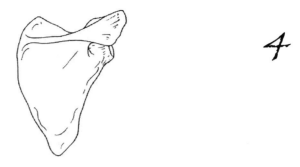

4

Navigating the Bones

I arrive back among the cool canopies of Tallahassee, ready to resume coursework. My semester will consist of five courses: Proseminar, a required course that prepares us for graduate coursework; Archaeological Conservation, where I will learn the techniques for preserving and conserving archaeological specimens such as human bone, wooden tools, and ancient fabrics; Seminar in Cultural Anthropology, one of my "core" courses, an examination of aspects of human culture from around the world; Museum Object, one of my Museum Studies courses that teaches the fundamentals of museum exhibition and design; and, most important of all, Human Osteology. Here I will learn every aspect of the human skeleton so that I can proceed to Advanced Human Osteology in the spring, during which time I will learn how to analyze and interpret human remains. It will be a grueling semester but I am braced for the challenge. Not only will I be concentrating on skeletal analysis; I will also be preparing for my return to London and my internship within the Human Origins Programme next summer. The work begins.

When I was in grade school, my class took a trip to historic St. Augustine, Florida. Prior to Ponce de Leon's arrival in 1513, the area was home to the Timucuan Indians for almost three thousand years. The city of St. Augustine was established by Don Pedro Menendez in 1565 and is the oldest continually occupied city in the United States. The rough, bricked streets affront centuries-old homes that stand in the shadow of the magnificent Castillo de San Marcos, the coquina-walled fort that was built in 1695 and still bears the faint graffiti of soldiers held within its walls.

We spent the day touring sites, learning about the history of the Spanish incursions in early Florida. Our last stop was the famed Fountain of Youth, the source of restorative waters that legend claims de Leon was searching for when he stumbled onto Florida. For the past three hundred years, the area around the Fountain was home to farms and citrus orchards. In 1901, Dr. Louella Day McConnel arrived, buying up the property and charging admission to all who were interested in drinking the clear, cool water flowing from her spring.

When my class visited the site, you passed through an open-air structure that held panels of information concerning the age of the site and its mythical history. There were cheesy photos of the Spanish eagerly approaching the Fountain, jockeying for a place in order to douse themselves with the restorative waters. I remember little about the fountain. What I remember are the skeletons.

Long before the passage of the Native American Graves Protection and Repatriation Act (NAGPRA) in 1990 and the subsequent heightened sensitivity toward the exhibition of Native American skeletal remains, the Fountain of Youth contained an exposed burial ground where one could peer down from an elevated walkway at a cemetery in which the bones had been exposed. Known as "pedestalling" in archaeological terms, the dirt covering the bones had been removed, the skeletons exposed in the positions in which they were buried.

What I saw were the remnants of individuals who had lived thousands of years in the past, their remains now viewed by curious tourists and, in my case, an awestruck child. I couldn't believe what I was looking at. Skeletons that at one time lived, breathed, ate, and slept so long ago; individuals performing all the mundane tasks that people perform today on a daily basis. These skeletons had actually been alive but were now reduced to bones in the ground. That fact was hard for me to get my young mind around. My teacher finally pried my hands from the guardrail. As we were herded back to the awaiting buses, I quickly swiped a brochure from one of the information racks so that I would have a photo of the cemetery. I stared at it all the way home and for several days afterward. Although this experience was my initiation into the fascinating world of archaeology, it wasn't the first time I had been captivated by skeletons. My obsession began with a parrot.

I was only seven years old, living in the Philippines with my parents, siblings, and our myriad of pets. One of these pets, a large green parrot, was the bane of my mother's existence. The parrot was an ill-tempered bird, aptly named Polly, despite his status as an unruly male. He was loud, argumentative, and prone to screeching at the most inopportune times, such as when my father attempted to bless our meals or late in the evening when the light was fading from the sky and my mother finally had a chance to relax from a day of noise and children. Polly would let out a loud screech and my mother would resort to her usual threats of throttling the bird and happily disposing of its carcass. One day, her wish came true. She phoned my father at his office, elatedly announcing, "The parrot's dead!"

The funeral was held that evening. Polly was wrapped in toilet tissue and ceremoniously placed in a shoebox. We assembled in the backyard next to a small hole my father had dug before dinner and the bird was laid to rest with little fanfare. We said our goodbyes, my father quickly filling the hole as my mother bounced back into the house.

That should have been the end of it. We had many more pets to attend to but for some reason, I became obsessed with Polly. I wasn't really obsessed with the bird itself; I was obsessed with what would become of his bones. I sat in my room that night, imagining Polly's feathered form being rapidly reduced to a skeleton by the industrious worms and beetles of my imagination. I had to see it.

The next morning, I begged my father to let me dig up the parrot, certain I would find a beautiful skeleton in the shape of a bird that I could mount in my room. My father, being better acquainted with rates of decomposition, refused my request, along with the numerous requests I pestered him with for the next few days.

I was never permitted to dig up Polly. But the death of that annoying bird had sparked a fascination with bones that I have held throughout my life. Rarely do I drive by a clump of road kill without craning my neck in order to identify the victim. One of my childhood dreams was to stumble upon a human skeleton while playing in the woods. What drama, what intrigue! I've been addicted to bones ever since.

The skeleton has played a vital role in comparative studies tracing human origins and the evolution of life on earth. Some of the earliest evolutionary studies were based on embryologic observations – the different stages an embryo passes through on its way to full-term development. What these early researchers realized was that there were striking physical similarities in the stages that various organisms, especially mammals, reach during development. At certain stages – whether you are a chicken, a rabbit, a salamander, a tortoise or a human being – our embryos, especially in the early stages, look very much the same.

Our evolutionary examination of human beings depends solely on the skeleton: either bones, teeth, or, when possible, DNA extracted from either. By comparing changes in size, morphology, and function, we can determine relationships between and among species going back millions of years.

So today begins my official entry into the world of human skeletal analysis, or bioarchaeology. Class work is split between lecture and lab. Lectures take place in a classroom and, across the hall, lab will be held in the secured room housing the remains from Windover. They will serve as our primary teaching collection. Few students in the country have the privilege of working on so ancient a population. Their extraordinary preservation combined with the broad population profile (meaning the population includes individuals of all age groups) provides us with opportunities to examine health throughout the many stages of life.

But first we must learn how to identify every bone in the human body, determine which side of the body it came from, and be able to name every fossa, fissure, suture, and landmark. This will enable us to distinguish human bone from animal; identify even the smallest bone fragments and determine from which part of the body they came; separate individuals who have become "comingled"; and eventually determine the age, sex, and height of the individual in life.

There are typically 206 bones in the human body. These bones are articulated via 200 joints and 600 muscles. It is a complex framework critical to the maintenance of overall health. Its most obvious function is to provide structure and protection. The skeleton is overlain by skin and cartilage and propelled through the action of muscles. Many of our organs are encapsulated and suspended from within. Our brains are protected by our skulls. When injured, the brain can swell and literally be strangled by the unyielding vault of the cranium. Our ribs protect our fragile lungs and heart, but can also turn deadly when damaged. Broken ribs can rupture vessels or tear holes in the lungs, leading to collapse. Our pelvic bones protect our lower organs, but when crushed can lead to rapid blood loss and death. The skeleton's strength and durability can turn deadly when damaged or broken.

We start with the skull and work downward. The human skull has eighty-one individual landmarks that serve as points from which measurements are taken. These measurements, known as craniometrics, can then be used to determine ancestry as well as changes in shape and size of the skull over time. They are entered into statistical databases that match their dimensions to those from populations around the world, since people with common origins tend to have similarly shaped heads. Thus we are able to determine population origins and track movement of populations across space and time. These measurements can also be used to gauge change in skull shape over time, such as the reduction in jaw size that has taken place throughout our evolutionary past. With the advent of fire and the increased processing of the foods we eat, our jaws have actually shrunk compared to our early ancestors. This is why dentists make a good living extracting the "wisdom teeth" (our third molars) from a large percentage of the population; in many of us, our shrinking jaws can no longer accommodate a full set of teeth.

As the semester proceeds, we make our way down the body. We move from the head down the spine, discerning the different types of vertebrae that make up the spinal column; the delicate cervical vertebrae that form the neck; the larger thoracic verts, with their prominent spinous processes that form the ridges visible down the back you bend to touch your toes; and the clunky lumbar vertebrae, with their wide surfaces enabling them to bear the weight of the torso. The spine eventually tapers to the sacrum, that rectangular block of fused vertebrae that, along with the pelvic bones, makes up the pelvic girdle. At its terminal end are the miniscule coccyx bones, remnants of our ancestral tail.

The bones of the chest and pelvis are tackled next. We learn to order the ribs based on their shape and size. We also memorize the complex structure of the shoulder girdle, with its peculiar marriage of clavicle, scapula, and humerus. The strangely shaped bones that make up the pelvis are crucial to understanding our unique mode of locomotion (bipedalism) as well as discerning males from females. The architecture of the pelvis is dictated by our gate and our sex, with the high, narrow orientation of the male pelvis contrasted with the bowl-shaped, wider version of the females'; both of them differ dramatically from our four-legged (quadruped) ancestors.

Finally, we work our way down the arms and legs and find ourselves grappling with the myriad bones that make up the hands and feet. Not only are they numerous, with seven bones composing the foot and eight the hand; the bones that make up the fingers and toes are similar in shape and size, making them tricky for someone with an untrained eye to distinguish. There's nothing more embarrassing than placing a skeleton in proper anatomical order, only to find you've confused the bones of the fingers and toes.

As the semester draws to a close, I now can name, identify, and side every bone in the body. I can name every landmark on the skull. I can even identify small fragments of an individual, a skill essential for any bioarchaeologist, since recovering an entire skeleton in the archaeological record is a rare occurrence. I am now ready to move on to Advanced Osteology, where I will apply this knowledge to assessing the age, sex, and height of an individual, as well as identify any pathological processes they experienced in life. It's about to get really interesting.

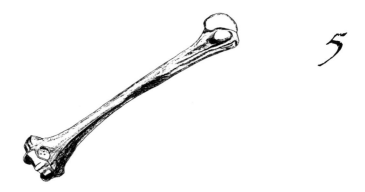

5

Interpreting the Bones

The semester ends, we break for the holidays, and in no time January arrives and the spring semester is under way. Since most of my energies will be focused on skeletal analysis, I'm taking only three courses: Seminar in Archaeology – a graduate course in archaeological theory; Linguistics – another of my "core" courses and supposedly a killer; and Advanced Osteology, in which I will learn to determine the physical attributes of an individual. Let's return for a moment to the burial of the young boy at Windover pond.

At the time of his death, he was around eighteen years of age. It was a hard life. During his embryological development, the bones of his lower spine failed to fuse around his spinal cord, leaving it exposed and prone to infection. His condition, known as spina bifida, is fairly common; it occurs in about ten percent of people in any given population. Its cause is still uncertain – possibly genetic, possibly infectious, but it left him facing an uphill battle for the remainder of his short life. Paralyzed, his legs were shriveled from non-use, what doctors call "disuse atrophy." He had massive infection in his right leg and it appears at some point in life, his foot had slowly rotted away, further ensuring his inability to walk. His teeth indicate he experienced periods of nutritional stress, perhaps secondary to the infection that slowly spread throughout his body and his lower spine curved to the right in a subtle case of scoliosis. He died before he was twenty.

How do we know so much about him? We know through the examination and analysis of his skeleton. The bones serve as guides to past lives. They are the best source of information we have concerning the life, health, and death of past peoples.

Let's take a brief walk through the analysis of his skeleton. He was part of a commingled burial, probably the result of several burials merging over time as the base of the pond shifted. The first task is to separate his remains from the others. This is done by looking at the size of the bones, the approximate age of the individuals, and the general condition of the bones, since bones will deteriorate depending on how long they have been in the ground and what the surrounding environment was like. In the case of the pond, the color of the bones will vary depending on their depth, location in the pond, and exposure to sunlight.

Fortunately, he was the only teenager among the six in which he was commingled, so it is fairly straightforward to distinguish him from the others. Next, the bones are assembled in anatomical order and laid out on a table where and an inventory is taken: in his case, a relatively complete skeleton with the exception of the right foot. Then the actual analysis begins.

Age is determined in adult remains based on changes that take place on the surfaces of certain bones, primarily those of the pelvis. The joint surfaces where the sacrum joins the pelvic bones (the sacroiliac joint) and where the pelvic bones come together in front (the pubic symphysis) provide the ideal surfaces to gauge how old someone is because their surface texture changes as an individual ages. These surfaces go from being smooth and nonporous when young to increasingly roughened and porous the older the person gets. They also develop elevated rims of bone at their edges. Each of these changes are assessed and compared to standards that provide an approximate age at time of death. But these aren't the only indicators of age.

When a child is born, the newborn can pass its bulbous head through the narrow birth canal only because of the flexibility of an unfused skull. If the bones of the skull were already fixed in place at the time of birth, a woman's hips would have to be much wider than they typically are in order for the head to pass (a feature no woman would eagerly embrace). This is why newborns have a "soft spot," that flexible area on the top of their skull where the plates of the skull are joined by connective tissue. By the age of two, the bones will join to form a suture, one of many composing the skull. As a person ages, these sutures eventually fuse to such a degree they disappear; they become "obliterated." A person's age can be assessed by the degree of closure of each suture. Landmarks around the skull are scored based on the degree of closure – on the outside of the skull, on the interior surface, and on the roof of the mouth (the palatine sutures). Although not a highly accurate means of aging an individual, it is best when used in conjunction with other means of age assessment.

The ribs also provide information as to age. The sternal ends of the ribs, where they are joined via cartilage to the sternum, change with age just like the surfaces of the pelvis. Flat and smooth when a person is young, over time they develop bony spicules that encircle the rib's end. The surface itself becomes porous and roughened. The skeleton, just like our skin, is affected by the aging process and becomes a complex landscape of roughened, porous growth.

Determining the age of a child at the time of death uses different techniques because many of the bony changes used for adult age assessment do not present until later in life. The long bones of the arms and legs can be measured and compared to standards in order to determine how much growth has taken place during the life of the child. But the most common technique is based on the teeth. Teeth, both deciduous (baby) and permanent, erupt at known rates within a child's life. At the time of birth, the teeth are forming within the jaws of the child. The front teeth start erupting at around six months of age; the molars, around eighteen months. The first permanent teeth emerge around six years of age, the first molars leading the way. Eruption rates allow us to assess the age of the child at death based on which teeth have emerged within the jaws.

Aging an elderly skeleton can also be tricky. Beyond the age of fifty, bony changes on the landmarks used to gauge the age of the individual stabilize, since the surfaces can only deteriorate so far. Another unusual thing occurs: the skeleton of an elderly male becomes more gracile; those of elderly females can take on somewhat masculine features, especially around the face and jaw. Thus the elderly can be a bit more challenging to "sex," especially in the absence of a complete skeleton.

Once the age of the person is determined, next comes sex. If you have a complete adult skeleton, you can determine the sex of the individual with about ninety percent accuracy. That's because the size and shape of the skull and pelvis are determined by our sex. One of the primary roles of the skeleton is to provide attachment sites for our muscles. Because males typically have greater musculature, their skeletons tend to be more robust. A typical female skeleton will be more "gracile," less developed. Remember – there is tremendous variation among human skeletons so the techniques for skeletal analysis use multiple means of assessment to improve our accuracy and minimize mistakes.

When a person enters puberty, the changes in hormone levels trigger changes in the shape or morphology of the skeleton. Males tend to develop more masculine features in their face, which is typically accompanied by the sprouting of facial hair. The larynx or voice box descends, causing their voices to drop. Their musculature increases depending on their level of activity, which can cause additional changes in the skeleton. The larger the muscles, the more robust the skeleton since larger muscles need greater surface area on which to anchor.

For females, the hormonal changes of puberty prepare the body for pregnancy. The pelvis becomes more rounded and flared to improve the fetus's ability to pass through the birth canal. These changes are apparent in the skeleton. We put on body fat, our breasts become bigger (except in some cases like mine), all in preparation for pregnancy.

So, if an archaeologist is lucky enough to recover an adult skeleton with a skull and pelvis, sex can be determined with great confidence. Not so with children. The skeletal changes that accompany puberty are what enable us to discern males from females. That is why young boys can easily be disguised as girls; their skulls have yet to display the "typically male" traits that accompany adulthood. Prior to puberty, there is no truly reliable means of determining sex based solely on the skeleton. We typically record a child's skeleton as "ambiguous." If DNA can be extracted from the bones or teeth, sex can be determined based on genetics. But DNA can be tricky and expensive and is usually not part of a basic assessment unless you are fortunate enough to have the money and expertise to undertake molecular analysis.

The height or "stature" of the individual is valuable information as well. The height one achieves in life is not only determined by your genetics (tall parents typically mean tall children); it is also determined by an individual's health and the quality of their diet. Many studies assess the average height of populations, changes in height through time, and the relationship of height to a population's means of subsistence. Hunter-gatherer populations generally tend to have fewer health issues than agriculturalists. Their population numbers tend to be smaller (a group can get only so big if they are dependent on hunting), whereas agriculture usually accompanies denser populations living closer together. The more people you have living in one place, the greater the potential for issues of hygiene and the spread of disease. All of these issues can affect overall height of a population.

When the Spanish first encountered Native Americans in Florida, they noted the height of these tall natives. But everything is relative. The Spanish came from crowded cities where nutrition and hygiene issues left the majority of them shorter than the well-fed, healthy natives they countered in Florida. To add to the natives' mystique, Timucuan males wore their hair in top-knots, which added a few inches to their height, giving the impression of even greater stature compared to the vertically challenged Spanish. If you are ever in St. Augustine, check out the life-sized statue of Ponce de Leon in the city's square. He was quite petite.

So the age, sex, and height of an individual can be readily apparent on the skeleton. Even if the skeleton is fragmented (which most archaeological specimens are), recognizing the important landmarks on fragmented remains can provide information about the dead. Fragments of a skull can still be "sexed" or "aged." A piece of the jaw, say the angle of the jaw below the ear, is more sharply angled in males. A fragment of skull might contain a suture, from which level of "closure" can be assessed. A partial pelvis might exhibit a bit of the sciatic notch, which is wide in females, narrow in males. Every piece of bone recovered from an archaeological site has the potential for providing information about its owner. You just have to know how to read them.

But why do we do this? Why does it matter what sex, age, or height individuals are upon death? Why do we care about illness or injury in the past? What type of information can this provide? To answer these questions, let's take a brief look back in time, to when the analysis of human remains first came into focus.

Physical anthropology, now typically referred to as biological anthropology, dates back to the mid-nineteenth century. Even then, the field was divided among several specific areas of interest. Evolution, human origins, human variability, and its most insidious area – racial typology, all contributed to the field, as researchers searched to find meaning and order to the complex history of human beings. They felt the keys to our origins and the relationship of people throughout the world existed in our morphology. Skulls were measured and compared; people were categorized based on their outward appearance; and personal and mental attributes were then assigned to these classifications. Put all this information together and what do you get: racism on a grand scale.

It made perfect sense to many researchers: humans could be ranked, with (big surprise!) white Europeans on top, blacks on the bottom, and the rest of human kind stuffed somewhere in between. This ranking proved quite convenient. If certain races were considered "less than human," it was perfectly justifiable to rob them of their land, enslave them, and barter them like cattle. It also fueled the science of "eugenics," the belief that the inferior races should be extinguished and only those who possessed the desirable traits of intelligence, morality, and, most important of all, white skin, should be allowed to procreate. In marched the era of genocide; out came the deaths of millions.

Some of our earliest endeavors in physical anthropology proved to be less than stellar. But much of early science consisted of misguided attempts to understand the world around us. Over time, with greater understanding of human variability and the superficiality of this term "race," biological anthropologists have worked feverishly to dispute and destroy the early beliefs in racial superiority. As we have come to understand the close relationship of people throughout the world, the lines once separating us into racial categories have vanished, replaced by a clarified common thread.

Today, physical or biological anthropology continues to pursue multiple lines of evidence to understand our complex evolutionary history. And there are numerous lines of evidence which we can pursue. Once the basic traits of the individual are obtained, more sophisticated analyses are conducted, including identifying disease processes, examining heritable traits of the teeth, and conducting molecular analyses such as DNA and stable isotopes.

The assessment of pathologies can indicate overall health, nutritional quality of the diet, and disease prevalence within a population. Each individual is examined for signs of infection, nutritional stress, arthritis, and congenital abnormalities. Analyses of teeth indicate genetic relatedness, oral health, and diet. Wear patterns and dental disease help gain insight into the oral health of early populations and each are affected by diet. Included in this are the effects of using the teeth as tools, known as "extramasticatory use" (a good phrase with which to impress your friends).

DNA analysis allows comparisons within and between populations in order to determine genetic relatedness, population movement, and origins. Stable isotope analyses, specifically carbon, nitrogen, oxygen, and strontium provide information on diet, subsistence, territoriality, and resource utilization. The skeleton provides a vast array of information about who someone was and how he or she lived. If one knows how to read the bones, they are virtual guides to the past.

The sites themselves provide information about the environment, geology, and soils associated with cemeteries. The geoarchaeology of the site helps us understand how the site formed over time and what environmental changes have taken place since its deposition. By sampling locations within and around a site, radiocarbon dating can be used to determine how long a cemetery was in use.

Pollen recovered from sites allows paleoenvironmental reconstruction in order to better understand the environment at the time of usage and environmental changes that have taken place since the site's abandonment. Ceramics and tools associated with the burials can also be analyzed. Residue analyses can determine contents once held in ceramic vessels; use-wear analyses can determine whether tools were used prior to burial or were made specifically for interment and botanical remains are identified to determine plant use among ancient peoples. When taken together, the biological and environmental data can provide a comprehensive look at the interaction between ancient people and their environments.

So, if we return to our question "Why do we care about sex, age, height, and pathologies?" it is best explained by example. Picture a cemetery. The cemetery has been excavated and has produced the remains of fifty people. Analysis begins, and we determine the "demographic profile" of the population, meaning the sex and age of the each individual. Based on the number of males and females and the age distribution within the cemetery, hypotheses can be formed about the cemetery itself.

For example . . . say the cemetery is composed primarily of young males, all bearing traumatic injuries such as broken bones, head injuries, and missing limbs. What do you think could have caused such a scenario? War, perhaps?

Here's another. That same cemetery produces high numbers of children and elderly. Instead of in individual graves, all are interred together in a single mass grave. What do you think? An epidemic, perhaps?

You see, every aspect of a burial tells a story. These are highly simplified examples of a very complex process of excavation, analysis, and interpretation. But it is meant to get you thinking in terms of "information." Every cemetery, whether it holds one individual or one hundred, presents vital information about the past. By determining the composition of a cemetery, we can answer questions concerning its history and the life histories of those within.

What was the average age at death? What types of pathologies did the people encounter during life? Do the individuals display evidence for nutritional stress? Are their traumatic injuries indicative of violence? If so, is the violence concentrated in either sex? How tall was the average person? What were they buried with? How are the bodies arranged? Are children buried among the adults? This information is essential to our understanding of the past. And it's fascinating!

The semester is flying by, and I'm to the point where I can "sex" a skeleton from across the room, just by observing the features of the face. With each week, I'm spending more and more time with the skeletons from Windover. They have become familiar, like the well-worn pages of my favorite books. I spend a lot of time in the lab by myself. It's easier to work when the only other people in the room are the silent skeletons of seven thousand years ago; they are much more cooperative than the individuals I worked on in my past life as a paramedic.

I think about their lives. When I look at their faces, I try to imagine life in ancient Florida. How did they deal with the oppressive heat of summer; the thick swarms of mosquitoes that increase exponentially when the sun goes down; the hurricanes that sweep the peninsula in early fall? How difficult life must have been for them. Their teeth alone are enough to send shivers down your spine. They were plagued with dental disease. Tooth loss and infection permeate the jaws that line the shelves of the collection. But worst of all is the attrition.

Dental attrition, or the "wearing down" of teeth, is common among prehistoric populations. Among the people of Windover, high levels of grit in their diet along with the habitual use of their teeth as tools wore down even the baby teeth of children. Their small teeth display the flattened surfaces similar to those of the adults. If the child lived long enough, their worn-down baby teeth would be replaced by fresh permanent teeth, only to be worn down as the child matured. Many of the teeth were reduced to flattened nubs if the individual was fortunate enough to make it into their forties. The pain they must have experienced can only be imagined. But dental disease wasn't the only health issues they faced.

Traumatic injury was also prevalent. My accident-prone years in the Philippines left me intrigued by trauma. In my career as a paramedic, trauma patients were my favorite. Each one is like a jigsaw puzzle; they have been damaged in countless ways, their bodies sometimes in pieces. My job as a medic was to determine the type of injuries, their extent within the body, and the method of stabilization and treatment in order to improve their chances of survival.

Gleefully did I respond to the frequent gunshot wound; happily did I bounce from the truck on the scene of high speed collisions. Whenever I was dispatched to a trauma call, my heart would leap at the possibility of multi-system trauma. An entrapped patient within a mangled car; a knife fight that turned deadly; each call had me champing at the bit, anxious to get to the patient and begin treatment.

I think my fascination with trauma is linked to my fascination with the skeleton, since traumatic injury typically involves the skeleton. Whether it's a gunshot wound, an automobile crash, or a fall from a height, usually bone will be impacted. The bullet will shatter bone in its path; the unrestrained driver's chest will be smashed by the steering wheel; the suicide attempt from the fifth floor will crush whichever side of the skeleton on which they land. Each traumatic incident has the potential for engaging the skeleton in a myriad of bone-shattering ways. It was my job as a medic to put the patient back together; to stabilize them for transport to a trauma facility where the hands of the surgeons would carefully reconstruct the broken pieces.

So as I work my way through Advanced Osteology, I'm thinking of the future. I'm thinking about my thesis. I'm thinking about trauma. What better way to engage my love of trauma than to assess the types and frequencies of traumatic injuries among the people from Windover. The only thing more interesting to me than traumatic injury today is traumatic injury that took place over seven thousand years ago. I've just found my thesis topic.

But before I can begin data collection, the semester winds to a close, and I'm preparing for my return to London. It's back to the Natural History Museum; not as a visitor, but as an intern. My internship will serve as a passport into the extensive hidden world of their collections, where I'll work with original and casts of specimens that lived millions of years ago. I'm entering the Museum's Department of Paleontology.

6

Bones in a London Basement: The Natural History Museum

I walk into the museum on my first day of internship, arriving well before it opens. I'm admitted by security and ushered to the front desk, where my badge awaits. I'm then directed down a long corridor, the blackened fossils of ichthyosaurs and plesiosaurs eyeing me from the gallery walls as I head for a wooden, glass-paned door at its end. This small door will mark my entry into the Paleontology Department, where I'll spend the next two months doing . . . well, whatever they tell me to do. We have no projects outlined. I arrive with the ability to analyze human remains and a fairly solid background in museum studies, and that's about it. I don't know if I'll be analyzing remains or emptying the trash. I don't really care. All I care is that I'm here.

The Anthropology Collections are one of eighteen massive collections housed within the Paleontology Department. Most of the collections are familiar: Birds, Brachiopods, Echinoderms, and Fish. Some are complete mysteries: Machaeridia, Micropalaeo, and Trace Fossils (which I can only assume are really tiny fossils). I make a mental note to investigate the unknowns on the Internet.

Once I'm through the door, the Department opens up into an immense, dark, shelf-lined maze. I make my way along the outer perimeter to Stringer's office, not sure if I'm to check in with him or with Robert. They are both there, smiling and greeting me with offerings of tea. Robert takes me on a tour of the Collections, showing me the crucial areas such as the "toilet" and the break room. The break room is a small, crowded room stuffed with outdated tables and chairs, its counters lined with teapots and packages of "biscuits." I make a mental note of the biscuits for future reference.

Robert then takes me on a tour of the collections with which I'll be working. They have decided I'll begin with Dr. Stringer's hominid cast collection. Because of its value, it's housed within their office confines. White cabinets stretching from floor to ceiling house expensive casts of every specimen linking humans to our ancient primate relatives yet discovered. Most of these casts predate the computer-generated casts made today: a technique that has made cast production of even the most exclusive specimens reasonably affordable. Prior to these new techniques, good casts were almost as precious as the original specimens and only the most exclusive institutions possessed them.

Robert unlocks the cabinets one by one, revealing the blank stares of skulls that possess features similar to our own, yet retain those more primitive characteristics such as massive brow ridges, powerful jaws, and large bony crests on the top of their skulls from which massive muscles were once attached. The casts are housed in discolored paper and disintegrating padding. They will need to be repackaged in new materials, with updated labels. I know what you're thinking – what an incredibly boring job! But the anal-retentive museum geek within me is delighted! Not only will I be working within the Human Origins Programme, I will actually be handling one of the most extensive hominid cast collections in the world, belonging to one of the most eminent human origins experts in the world. It doesn't get much better than this.

So I begin, carefully removing each precious skull from its shelf, slowly replacing the worn and faded wrappings with fresh paper, proper padding, and updated labels. The work is slow; I take my time. My biggest fear is accidentally drop-kicking one of the skulls across the room as I make my way from shelf to table. My hands tremble for the first day or so.

After a few days I settle into a routine. Each morning I saunter into the museum, proudly displaying my badge, hoping to be mistaken for museum personnel. The Department becomes a familiar backdrop. During lunch each day, I pick a new area of the museum to explore, taking in the immense collections and how they are displayed, wondering at the extent of these amazing objects. Being in the museum, I feel I'm learning through osmosis; just being surrounded by so much information, I can feel my knowledge base expanding. The language of science rolls from my tongue. My afternoons typically involve a covert mission into the break room, where I smuggle a handful of biscuits from the littered countertop.

I complete the hominid cast project and move on to the stone tool collection. Robert takes me through the immense collection, one of the largest ancient stone tool collections in the world. Some of them are millions of years old, collected from the parched African earth. I hold them as our ancestors did, my hand fitting perfectly into the tool's worn notches. The stones are large, teardrop shaped, and of varying earthy colors – pale peach, dusky rose, burnt orange – their color altered by fire. I picture their makers, huddled in the night under dark African skies, the sounds of hungry predators drawing close as the crack of stone on stone rings across the plains. To touch an object that was created long before humans ever ventured out of Africa is to be transported back to our humble beginnings, that remote period when humans were becoming human.

The Natural History Museum, London.

Amidst my projects, I also have opportunities to work with some of the museum's retired researchers. Peter Andrews, an expert on fossil apes, got his start in the field by working as a game warden in Africa, fortuitously under Louis Leakey, who urged him into the field of paleoanthropology. Although retired, Peter, like many retired researchers at the museum, retains an office and works among the collections as if he had never left. These ambitious researchers can't be slowed down by a little thing like retirement. I work with Peter on his cast collection of primate fossil teeth. Days are spent organizing and labeling his collection as he explains the differences in primate teeth in relation to our own; late afternoons are spent sipping brandy in his office as I listen to his amazing tales of Africa.

My skeletal training comes in handy when Theya Molleson, a retired bioarchaeologist tracks me down within the collections one day to assign me a data collection project among the famed Spitalfields skeletons. Excavated between 1984 and 1989 from vaults beneath Christ Church in central London, almost one thousand skeletons, many of known age and identity, now line the shelves of the basement within the Paleontology Department. The burials took place between 1729 and 1859. Because the individuals were accompanied by personal information, many in the form of engraved plates affixed to their burial vaults, I have an opportunity to test various methods of determining age at time of death, since results can be verified by the written records.

Theya has me examining aspects of the pelvic bones for scars of parturition – supposed notches that form on the underside of the pelvis as a result of pregnancy. These scars have been the focus of controversy among bioarchaeologists. I am to examine large numbers of females in order to score for presence or absence of the scars to determine whether they truly indicate previous pregnancy or not. Since these scars can sometimes appear on the pelves of females who have never given birth, they are considered rather questionable as determinants for past pregnancy.

Theya also has me collect metric data for separate studies she is conducting so I spend much of my days measuring skeletons. Each morning I report to her office, where she gives me instructions for the day. I haul my equipment (computer and measuring instruments) down into the basement and get to work. It's wonderful to have the opportunity to work on this famous collection, but the work is isolating. The basement where all

Bones lining the dark tunnels of *Le Catacombs*, Paris.

the skeletal material is stored is composed of large, rolling shelves that move along tracks. When not in use, the shelves are pressed together and locked in place. I wonder to myself how long it would take them to find me, should I accidently crush myself between the sliding shelves. At least I would have the company of the people from Spitalfields.

Theya is well-known for her work among the skeletons from Çatalhöyük, a nine-thousand-year-old site in Turkey. She identified small indentations on the bones of many of the women's feet, caused from constant squatting while grinding grain. These "squatting facets" are one of many indications of repetitive action that show up on the skeleton, wearing down surfaces, eroding joints.

Since I'm living at the FSU IP facility again, I have the opportunity to travel with the current museum studies students as they head to Paris for the weekend. I'm anxious to return to the beautiful city, primarily for one reason: *Le Catacombs*.

When I was in Paris last summer, *Le Catacombs* were closed for renovation. I'm determined to make it in this time. As soon as we arrive in Paris, I split from the group and head downtown. I arrive at the small, nondescript entrance and head inside, only to be informed it is closing early. I plead with the man behind the county, explaining that this is my second attempt to see this spectacular display of human remains. He takes pity on me, waving me inside as he places a chain across the entrance behind me. I'm in!

Le Catacombs date back to the eighteenth century. As Paris grew in size and population, burial within consecrated ground became increasingly hard to come by. To make matters worse, "The Black Death" swept north through Europe, reaching Paris in the 1300s. Carried by infected fleas on the rats that inhabited the city, it annihilated the population of Paris, killing approximately 800 per day, leaving 50,000 dead in its wake. Eventually, only the wealthy could afford to be buried within church cemeteries; the rest of the population was relegated to the communal plots where they were disposed of en mass, their bodies sprinkled with lime to aid in decomposition. Once thoroughly decomposed, the bones would be removed to make way for additional burials and placed in "chaniers," or charnel houses that lined the communal plots.

There were several problems with this process. For one, the mass graves were so overcrowded that the decomposing bodies were leaching into the ground, contaminating nearby wells. Second, the charnel houses, which continued to be built in order to keep up with the steady flow of bones, were soon overflowing as well. Something had to be done.

Alexandre Lenoir was the first to propose using the vast network of abandoned mine shafts that snaked beneath the city's streets. The idea took hold and for two years, beginning in 1786, nightly processions of wagons filled with human remains were discreetly carted through the city led by chanting priests who oversaw their relocation. Today, over six million individuals line the dark corridors of *Le Catacombs*, all neatly arranged in imaginary patterns; endless stacks of femurs, long bones arranged like cordwood, and skulls lined up like books along the dank walls.

I make my way down the narrow, winding staircase that takes me below the city. I am alone, the rest of the visitors having exited prior to

Stacked bones within *Le Catacombs*.

closing. The only sound is the dripping of water as it seeps through cracks in the ancient walls. The passageway is lit by faint bulbs that cast a patchwork of shadows along the walls and the entire place smells like a damp sponge. It's much more extensive than I imagined. It's hard to fathom the number of individuals interred; the millions of bones housed within the mine's dark recesses. I snap pictures as I go, wanting to take the images with me, knowing I cannot possibly take this all in.

I spend an hour wandering the passageways, thinking about the lives represented by the remains within. I imagine Paris hundreds of years ago, wondering how many of these individuals succumbed to the plague, their bodies ravaged by the weeping sores and fever that killed about 80 percent of those infected. How they must have suffered. I make my way up the final staircase and out into the sunny brilliance of late afternoon.

I spend the rest of the afternoon at the city's Museum of Natural History, with its long halls strewn with the suspended bones of extinct creatures. Giant sharks and whales careen overhead; an enormous alligator snarls from beyond the rope barrier, poised to attack. And tucked in a corner at the end of the hall is an exquisite collection of human fetal skeletons, all of them conjoined twins who stare out from the cloudy glass jars that house their remains. Some are joined at the chest (thoracopagus); some are joined at the head (craniopagus); some share a single body with two heads emerging from the shoulders (dicephalic). Each of them represents the wonders of embryology and the haunting results of development gone awry.

When not working on my projects, I am writing a paper on the history of the Museum. This paper will serve as my final project for my internship. It recounts the museum's origins, the evolution of its collections, and the current educational programs it conducts to engage the public. One of these is an adult field trip to the southern coast of England to view the Triassic folds in the shoreline. I immediately sign up.

The trip leaves from the museum early Saturday morning. There are about twenty of us; most are London residents but a few are tourists, some from as far away as Australia. The bus takes us south, and a few hours

Standing atop the cliffs overlooking the southern coast of England.

later we arrive at the beautiful cliffs of southern England. The small village where we are dropped is set among rolling fields of flowers, and the brisk wind off the ocean is laced with their scent. The shore is far below; we head down a steep, narrow path, picking our way through rock and loose dirt as we follow our guide. He is a retired geologist. He carries an old walking stick and spits when he talks. We follow, all of us in brightly colored hard hats to protect our fragile skulls from tumbling boulders.

We end up on a narrow, pebble-strewn beach. Facing the shore, the stony cliffs rise over a hundred feet behind us. The wind on the beach whips along the shoreline, smelling of sea salt and grass. Shorebirds rush among the rocks, racing the waves up and down the beach as they search for small creatures among the foam. And in the distance, the white, chalky cliffs of the Isle of Wight stand out in contrast against the blue of the Celtic Sea.

Our guide draws our attention to the dramatic layers of folding earth that rise above our heads. These rocks were laid down over 200 million years ago, their layers compressed over immense time. They ripple throughout the cliffs, the folds the result of shifting land masses, and drifting continents. The face of the cliff is worn by millions of years of salt, wind, and sand. It is smooth to the touch.

Our guide, a geologist explaining the ancient formations along the coast.

We spend the afternoon climbing along the shore, as our guide spits his way through the geological history of England. I collect small stones that have been worn smooth from years of tumbling in the surf. Some of them are broken; their inner cores reveal beautiful shades of pinks and corals. As the afternoon sun slants to the west, we head back up the cliff to make our way back to London. It has been a wonderful day of sun and wind; an escape from the darkness of the Museum's basement and the grit of the city. It marks my final weeks of internship as the summer wanes and the fall semester approaches.

Upon my return to FSU, another grueling semester awaits. But I won't spend this one huddled over books, or poring over notes in a classroom. I will attend a nine-credit-hour course where I will learn every aspect of archaeological investigation: remote sensing, topographic mapping, gridding, excavating, sorting, and analyzing all that we find during our field school. This fall, I become an archaeologist.

An Introduction to Dirt

Archaeology is one of the four sub-fields within Anthropology. Along with linguistics, physical (or biological) anthropology, and cultural anthropology, archaeology offers a multidisciplinary approach to the study of human beings. Archaeology focuses on material culture. Artifacts are any items that have been modified by humans, such as tools, weapons, pottery, and utensils. Archaeology encompasses all evidence of human presence and often includes other lines of evidence, such as the plants (botanical) and animals (faunal) utilized by man.

Archaeology has developed its own sub-specialties. Prehistoric archaeologists deal with sites that predate the written word. In North America, these include all sites before European contact, since Native Americans in North America lacked written language. Historic archaeologists deal with sites that post-date the written record. Written records are frequently used to corroborate what is found in the archaeological record. At times, evidence from the ground can contradict or disprove historic accounts. As they say, "History is written by the winners"; what we read in the history books doesn't always reflect what actually took place.

Underwater archaeologists deal with sites that were originally or have since become submerged. These include shipwrecks, which in Florida literally lace the state's vast coastline; and habitation sites, most of them located in the Gulf of Mexico, which have since become submerged due to rising sea levels that followed the end of the last ice age.

Our field school class meets each morning before dawn, behind the Department of Anthropology, where we load our field equipment into the dilapidated departmental van. The van is battered and white and resembles a dead whale that has been tumbled in the surf. The bulk of the equipment has already been taken to the site, which is known as the Castro Site after the family that owns the large, sprawling farm on the outskirts of town. Their land just may hold evidence for a Spanish mission that, according to historic documents, was located in the vicinity. It is our job to find it.

There are about fifteen of us, plus two field crew leaders and our instructor, Dr. Rochelle Marrinan. Marrinan is a historic archaeologist who has spent years in the field under the scorching Florida sun, hunting for traces of early Spanish sites. She is petite, with boy-short hair and a perpetual tan. She is fiercely direct, her tongue a blunt weapon in moments when she's tired or aggravated.

She and I share a lot in common. She was a nurse for many years before switching gears and entering a graduate program at the University of Florida. We chat about our medical pasts as we drive out to the field each day. Marrinan also instructed me in my Paleonutrition course. A gifted zooarchaeologist, she can identify the species of animal from the most minute fragments; a bit of vertebrae, a tiny piece of jaw.

FSU's archaeological field school is unique. Most field schools take place in the summer and last for about a month or two. FSU offers a full semester of field work – a rare opportunity to work for three months learning every aspect of site investigation. We will begin by mapping an area on the outskirts of the site, testing it for suitability for future studies. We will then move down the pasture to the main site, where we will open up large area, sifting through mountains of dirt in hopes of finding some small trace of the Spanish as they passed through the area hundreds of years ago.

The farm is a vast expanse of grass and cattle. It has been in the family for several generations, each one tending the large herds and fertile acres on which they graze. The family has been kind enough to allow our team to excavate an area toward the back of their property. Here, we students will learn all the ins and outs of archaeological excavation.

We spend the first week of the semester addressing the logistics of excavations. The rest of the semester will be spent in the field. We have field manuals and are given small, sturdy notebooks within which we will keep daily logs of our work and progress. We are expected to record daily weather conditions, assignments, and detailed daily summaries of our activities. These notebooks will be housed within the Anthropology Collections, archived with the artifacts recovered during our semester.

Marrinan has chosen an area high on a hill to investigate before we begin excavations. The area is singled out for its elevation, since these areas are most desirable for living sites. We will "test" the area via topographic mapping, remote sensing, and shovel testing.

Topographic mapping produces a three-dimensional map of an area. Data is collected by a "total station," a small computer on stilts from which a laser beam is directed onto a target at the top of a pole held by personnel at a distance from the station. As the person holding the target moves throughout the area, the computer takes incremental readings, capturing their distance and elevation. These data are then manipulated via special mapping programs to produce topographic, or contour, maps of an area. These maps provide a lay of the land, showing elevations and depressions on the landscape which assist in identifying possible sites.

Remote sensing utilizes ground penetrating radar (GPR) to record "anomalies" within the ground. The anomalies can be metallic objects or simply variations in soil composition. A map of the anomalies is produced and can be integrated into the topographic data, producing distributions of anomalies throughout an area. We lay out a grid prior to shovel testing. Florescent flags mark the locations across the grid where testing will take place, say every meter or five meters, depending on the size of the area and the available time and personnel. Testing pits that produce artifacts will be highlighted. The resulting information is married to the topographic map and remote sensing data, and what emerges is a landscape marked by artifact clusters and underground anomalies – each of which could be part of a larger archaeological site. These data provide a means of surveying an area without the time and labor of a full-scale excavation.

When the survey is complete and Marrinan is satisfied with the amount of data, work shifts to the main site. She and her students have been working here for the past two years, collecting evidence for Spanish presence in the area.

We open up a large area, carefully removing the overburden of grass and weeds. We then proceed downward, ten centimeters at a time, mapping anything obvious in the ground, such as artifacts or "features" – ephemeral changes in soil composition or color which can indicate an ancient structure or event (such as trash deposition). The dirt removed from the "unit" is transported via wheel barrows to one of several screens lined up along the periphery of the area. The dirt is dumped onto the screens and sprayed down, using garden hoses that snake beneath our feet. The water is used to force the soil through the screens. As the dirt is forced through, artifacts are caught in the screen, along with roots, seeds, and any critters that happened to have been living peacefully within the soil. When an artifact is recovered, it is bagged and labeled so that its "provenience" or place within the unit is recorded. This way, every object recovered can be traced back to its location within the site. At the completion of the field work, every artifact will be mapped, to provide a comprehensive overview of the site and its layout. Once you know how a site is laid out, where and how the artifacts are distributed throughout the site, you can interpret the site's use.

I enjoy the physical labor; spending thirteen years in the fire service requires a dedication to sweat and toil. But what I come to realize over the first few weeks of excavation comes as a shock: archaeological excavation is boring as hell!

The months I've spent in the lab, poring over those beautiful skeletons that provide such depths of information, make other aspects of archaeology seem mundane and monotonous. Working in the field, digging for days on end, only to find a miniscule glass bead or a chunk of pottery, is totally anticlimactic. I stand by as Marrinan and others get excited when we come upon a "feature" in the soil. But these features, to me, are merely boring stains in the earth. I can't make heads or tails of what they might have been. The glass beads are interesting but so few and far between that they can hardly make up for the amount of labor involved in their recovery. And above all, the information we so laboriously pull from the earth seems so limited, so ephemeral.

I know there are talented archaeologists who can examine a site, noting the subtle color or textural changes in the soil, envisioning the type of structure or activity that took place in the distant past, and composing elaborate stories as to their origins. But all I see is dirt! Unless there's a bone at the end of my shovel, I could care less.

This epiphany is disappointing. I expected to love archaeological excavation. That is why I am here; to become an archaeologist, travel the world, recover lost civilizations, and leave my mark via some extraordinary discovery. But what I really want to do is get back to the lab and study bones. Only by handling the bones of the long-dead do I truly feel a connection with the past. To hold the fragile remains of someone who lived thousands of years ago, seeing their lives reflected in the injuries or illnesses they encountered during life – that is what archaeology is all about!

So I keep shoveling earth, sifting through the multitude of buckets that arrive at my screen, and I count the days until field school is over. If it weren't for the spectacular scenery, the cool fall days with the sun on my back, and the invigorating routine of reporting to the farm each day, this whole experience would be a drag. But I take from it what I can and should; I've had the opportunity to learn various techniques of surveying a site; I've experienced the elaborate logistics involved in prepping, opening, and closing a site; and by the end of the semester, I will officially be a trained archaeologist and will eventually apply these skills to the excavation of human remains.

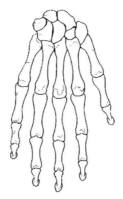

8

Body Bags and Floating Heads: Doing Time at the Pound Lab

Although field school has consumed most of my time, I have also been granted an "assistantship," a paid student position within the Department of Anthropology. Since I am working on my Museum Studies certification, I will serve as Collections Manager of the Department's Anthropology Collections. Aside from working in Collections, I have also begun data collection for my thesis. The topic of my research will focus on the type, frequency, and distribution of skeletal fractures among the Windover population. My fascination with traumatic injury has made me curious about the type of traumatic injuries the people of Windover experienced in life. My analysis will consist of examining each bone in the Windover population, all 10,000 of them. I'd better get to work.

I've also been reading about war crimes and the application of forensic anthropology to cases of genocide and mass graves. As in paleopathology, I feel naturally drawn to the field. I miss the grittiness of working as a paramedic. Many of my patients' injuries were the result of violence. Gunshot wounds, stabbings, and beatings were regular occurrences in the neighborhoods in which I worked. We worked closely with law enforcement in such situations, so the interplay of international law and genocide that characterize war crimes has a familiar ring.

My interest has led me to a new contact. Dr. Michael Warren is the Assistant Director at the C.A. Pound Human Identification Lab at the University of Florida in Gainesville. A former paramedic himself, we became friends following emails I sent him, asking questions about his field experience dealing with mass graves in countries that include Bosnia, Serbia, and Kosovo.

The Pound Lab was founded in 1972 by Dr. William Maples, one of the early pioneers in forensic anthropology. Like bioarchaeology, forensic anthropology involves the analysis of human remains and utilizes the same techniques in obtaining information from the skeleton. The context distinguishes the two disciplines. Forensics deals with remains from "medicolegal" contexts, typically those involving criminal activity. It also includes mass disasters and, on occasion, historic cases of wrongful or indeterminate death. The Romanovs are a great example.

During the Russian Revolution of 1917, Tsar Nicholas II, his wife Alexandra, and their five children were placed on house arrest in a remote location outside of St Petersburg. In July of 1918, Bolshevik soldiers appeared at their door in the middle of the night and ushered the family, along with their attendants, into the basement where they were shot and killed, their bodies secretly buried in an unknown location. Seventy-three years later, nine bodies were exhumed from an abandoned well. By analyzing DNA extracted from the remains and comparing it to that of living relatives, scientists confirmed the bodies were those of the Romanovs and the mystery surrounding their disappearance was finally solved. The traumatic wounds still evident on their skeletons confirmed their violent deaths.

The Pound Lab provides identification of human remains for the majority of medical examiners in the state of Florida. They also contract with several federal agencies. When human remains are discovered, either they are brought to the lab by law enforcement, or trained personnel from the lab report to the scene. The scene is carefully processed (mapped and photographed), and the remains are collected and transported back to the lab for analysis.

Warren has offered me an independent study in forensics, if I'm willing to make a weekly trip of two hours each way down to Gainesville, where I will work alongside his students under the supervision of his Lab Director. I accept without hesitation. The experience of working in a forensics lab will enhance my thesis research, since much of forensics deals with traumatic injury on the skeleton. But my work at the lab won't be restricted to analyzing skeletons. I'll also be schooled in one of the more macabre aspects of forensic anthropology: defleshing a human body.

When I pull up under the giant oaks, I immediately notice the sweet, familiar odor of decaying flesh rising from the exhaust vents on the side of the building. I came to know that odor well during my tenure as a medic. We frequently responded to 911 calls from family or friends who hadn't seen loved ones or neighbors for several days. The police would receive the call, who in turn would notify the fire department, since we provided forcible entry into the residences. In cases where the individual had been dead for several days, the familiar stench of decay would greet us at the front door.

The small portable building on UF's campus that houses the Pound Lab is tightly secured. Because the majority of cases are part of legal investigations, chain of custody is mandatory in order to maintain the integrity of the evidence—the remains of victims.

The origins of forensic anthropology are credited to Thomas Dwight, who in the late 1800s focused on the analysis of human remains in medicolegal contexts. The application of his methods brought forensics into focus during the infamous Parkman murder case of 1849. John Webster was a chemistry professor at Harvard; Dr. George Parkman was a prominent physician. After borrowing money from Parkman, Webster decided it would be easier to kill Parkman than pay back the loan. Following the killing, he dismembered the body, distributing body parts among his lab and septic tank and burning Parkman's head in his furnace. Oliver Wendell Holmes and Jeffries Wyman, both anatomy professors at Harvard, were asked to gather the body parts, analyze the remains, and determine the identity of the victim. They were able to determine age, sex, and height, all of which matched Parkman. The final bit of evidence that sealed the case was a set of dentures found in Webster's furnace which just happened to match dental molds made by Parkman's dentist. Thus, forensic anthropology was born and John Webster was convicted.

Warren meets me for my first day, introduces me around the lab, and describes the work I'll be doing. The building consists of a few small offices and a single large room that serves as the heart of the lab. The lab is filled with tables strewn with the remains of individuals who either met an untimely end at the hands of an assailant or whose bodies were discovered abandoned and unidentified. They are in various states of completeness. Some are entire skeletons, their bones neatly arranged in anatomical order as students carefully examine each element. Some individuals are represented by just a few bones, their abandoned corpses having been scattered and partially consumed by scavengers.

Forensic anthropology has two primary goals: to identify the individual and to determine, when possible, the cause and manner of death. Identity is determined by assessing the skeleton, using the same methods as bioarchaeology; the sex, age, and stature of the individual. Forensics also assigns ancestry to the individual, conforming to law enforcement categories and narrowing down the search within missing persons databases.

Cause of death is determined by examining the skeleton for signs of trauma from intentional injury or for pathological processes that may have led to the natural death of the individual. Trauma analysis plays an integral role in forensics because death of a victim is usually the result of traumatic injury. This includes toxins and poisonings, which can leave their evidence within bone, hair, and fingernails.

When there is evidence for trauma, the next step is to determine when the injury occurred; this will assist in determining whether it was related to the cause of death. Did the injury occur prior to death (antemortem)? Did the injury occur around the time of death (perimortem)? Or did the damage occur after the individual was already dead (postmortem)? Perimortem injuries are of greatest interest to the forensic analyst, since they can be tied to cause of death. Postmortem damage includes weathering of the bone from exposure; natural breakage from the weight of soil; or damage from carnivores. These postmortem "alterations" that take place once the body is placed in the ground are known as "taphonomic" changes and make up a subspecialty within forensics.

The manner of death refers to how a person died. This can range from scenes of violence to natural causes. In forensics, there are five manners of death: homicide, suicide, accident, natural, and unknown. It is the job of forensics to determine to which category an individual is assigned.

Other vital bits of information include determining how much time has passed since the person died; whether the person died where they were found or the body was transported from another location; the collection of all evidence surrounding the victim, such as associated clothing (which may contain DNA of the assailant), weapons, and personal belongings; and the nature of interment, meaning how the body was buried – surface find, shallow grave, or formal burial. The type of burial can sometimes indicate the relationship between the assailant and victim; a body left on the surface indicates disregard for the victim; a formal grave may indicate some form of relationship between the two.

Forensics is a highly multidisciplinary specialty, and quality work depends on input from an array of specialists. Ballistics experts provide vital information concerning the nature of firearms and ammunition. Determining the direction, speed, and focus of projectiles such as bullets helps re-create the moments leading up to the injury; the position of the assailant in relation to the victim, the caliber of gun that was used, and the distance between the two. This information becomes critical when determining the chronology and scenario of events. When someone claims self-defense, the location of wounds on the victim or the path the trajectory took can make or break their case. A gunshot wound to the back of the victim's head doesn't bode well for claims of "self-defense."

Other specialists that contribute to forensic cases include forensic entomologists—those who specialize in the identification of insects in association with dead bodies. By determining the type of insects and the number of larval stages that appear on the body, they can determine the season in which the individual died and how long the person has been dead. Insects are generally seasonal and the succession of different types of bugs can provide a chronology for the amount of time that has passed. Blow flies always get there first, no matter the season. They are usually followed by beetles. Eventually the beetles outnumber the flies as the soft tissue is consumed. Thus, the ration of flies to beetles can be used to gauge time since death.

Forensic botany is another specialty involved in forensics. They help determine when a person died based on the type and extent of plant growth around the remains. Forensic odontologists, those specialists that provide identification based on the teeth, come in very handy in cases of severe burns and mutilating trauma that accompany mass disasters such as plane crashes. They also assist in cases of poor preservation, since sometimes the teeth are the only aspect of the skeleton left in the ground.

I work at the lab each Tuesday, reporting for duty at nine in the morning. Because of my student status, I will be working on old cases of unclaimed individuals housed in large brown shoeboxes pulled from the shelves lining the rear of the lab. I work through each case as if it has just arrived in the lab, assembling the remains, assessing them, and then composing a report of my findings. Knowing my interest in pathology, Warren chooses remains that exhibit various forms of illness or malnutrition in order to help me hone my skills in pathological assessment and identification. Following my assessment, I go over my findings with Warren or his Lab Director to gauge my accuracy. The first few weeks pass uneventfully. I work through each case, my findings becoming more accurate as the weeks go by.

When bones arrive at the lab, they are logged in under their case number and the analysis begins. But not everyone arrives at the lab already skeletonized. Some require a bit more processing.

She was a young female whose body had been found in the woods. Her age is assumed based on the tattered clothing that hangs from her decomposing body and the youthful appearance of her hands and feet. Her body bag has already been placed within the large vented containment shelf where disarticulation of decomposing individuals takes place. The containment shelf is a hooded work table with an evacuation system that sucks the foul-smelling air emitted from the corpse, releasing it to the outside. Lab personnel stand at the table, decked out in full containment suits with a glass partition protecting them from flying debris.

The body bag sloshes when we position it on the table; I dread looking inside. I'm working alongside the Lab Director, who will guide me through my first experience in defleshing a human being. She slowly unzips the bag.

We open the bag to find a thoroughly decomposing body within. It is unrecognizable; in fact, it's hard to discern we are even looking at a human being. The only indications are the pale, bloated hands and feet which have managed to stay relatively intact. We must wade into the slushy mess and extract her skeleton, which will be cleaned of remaining flesh and placed in a large pot where it will simmer with detergents for the next twenty-four hours in order to release the remaining fat from the bones, a process known as "maceration." It will then be laid out to dry on one of the examining tables where analysis can begin.

We go after the larger elements first, pulling from the slush the bones of her arms and legs. The ribs come out easily, her flesh completely broken down by the process of decomposition. Since her hands and feet are relatively intact, they must be squeezed in order to force out the small bones. We work them as if they were large tubes of toothpaste, the small bones falling onto the table as we milk each finger and toe. Pale pink polish is still visible on her fingernails.

Her spine is the most challenging. We must remove as much flesh as possible before she is macerated. We use small forceps to tear the remaining flesh from the convoluted surfaces of the vertebrae. It is frustratingly slow work. The flesh is slimy and tears easily. I wonder if this process will ever end!

The work is grueling, the smell awful. I keep a large biohazard trashcan next to me. Every few minutes, I lean over it, wracked with dry heaves. I've seen many decomposing bodies but have never had to handle them, feel their flesh slide between my fingers. It's a disgustingly surreal experience.

Working in the lab affords other opportunities as well. I learn techniques of radiography, how best to position remains to obtain X-rays that will be used in identification and documentation. Not all my subjects are skeletons; enter the floating head.

It was a bright sunny day off the coast of Florida when two fishing buddies set out on the open water for a day of sun and fun. As they threw back a few beers, poles in the water, a small object bobbed by their boat. It was a human head. They carefully scooped the head from the water, placing it in their cooler for safe keeping. Not wanting to waste a beautiful day, they continued to fish and eventually turned the head over to authorities late in the day, after they returned to shore. Needless to say, they were much maligned by the press and public for putting their desire to fish ahead of their civic duty. The head passed through various legal authorities before finally arriving at the Pound Lab for analysis and identification. My assignment: obtain a complete set of X-rays.

The head is a blackened mass of tissue, not really recognizable as a head. It's heavy. Its weight and level of decomposition make it difficult to position within the small radiography box used for X-raying body parts. The trickiest part is getting it to stand upright. Each time we set it inside the box, sliding the thick plexiglass cover down and stepping back to take the radiograph, the head slowly begins to tilt, eventually falling over with a dull thud. We finally prop it up with small Styrofoam boxes and are able to get the required shots. I'm relieved when the radiographs are complete and the head is returned to the cooler. I return to my casework as the weeks of the semester play out.

Working on forensic cases has a very different feel from working on archaeological remains. There is a sense of sadness to it. Archaeological skeletons from cemetery assemblages are typically individuals who lived their lives, most dying from some natural or environmentally induced cause; on rare occasions, from trauma or violence. But the skeletons of forensic cases run the gambit of tragedy. They are typically individuals who happened to be at the wrong place at the wrong time, or who associated with the wrong type of people. Many of them have been killed, their bodies dumped in remote locations for a lone hunter to stumble upon in the woods. Or they're the victims of mass disasters, such as plane crashes or savage storms. Or they were swept up in genocidal rampages, killed for their beliefs, ethnicity, or the color of their skin. They have typically met an untimely end, their only hope for identification placed in the hands of trained forensics experts. The Pound Lab makes me long for the clean, dry skeletons of Windover.

But working at the Pound Lab has provided another dimension to my assessment of human remains. I have completed my analysis of skeletal fractures among the Winodover population and now must compile the results of my thesis. Let the data crunching begin.

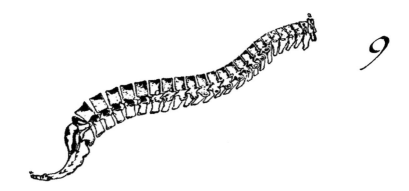

Broken Bones of Windover

The semester has been one of staring at bones. Whether in the Pound Lab, combing modern remains for evidence of trauma or pathology, or in the Windover lab, scouring bones and hunting for fractures, I'm developing the keen eye of a bioarchaeologist.

Patterns of injuries can provide clues to past events. High rates of trauma, especially among males exhibiting multiple injuries, can indicate interpersonal violence. Traumatic injury among females can indicate subordination to males. Fractures among children can indicate abuse.

Discerning the type of fracture can be problematic when the injury occurred years before death and the bone has had a chance to heal. As the bone mends, the "callus," that bony collar that forms around the break to afford stability as the bone heals, is "remodeled" and, if given enough time, can be resorbed by the body; all evidence of the injury disappears. This is especially true among children, whose rapid growth and higher rates of metabolism result in higher rates of bone "turnover" as old bone is replaced by new. Children's fractures can be completely erased much sooner than adult fractures.

The location of the fracture on the body can also be telling. Fractures to the head and face are typically indicative of violence, especially in the case of multiple wounds. Fractures to the forearms, known as parry fractures, may indicate defensive wounds as the individual lifts their arms to ward off a blow. Fractures can also be caused by repetitive use. Stress fractures are caused by consistent trauma and can be found in the hands, feet, and spine—any part of the body that is overused. Stress fractures of the feet are common injuries among runners.

Around 10,000 bones make up the 168 individuals from Windover. I inspect each bone one by one, searching for evidence of healing fractures. They range from obvious bulges on the bone's surface to trace lines depicting fractures in the individual's distant past. The children from Windover are especially challenging, since their active growth will have erased fracture lines completely, given enough time. Trauma assessments in bioarchaeology typically include only those fractures exhibiting some degree of healing, since postmortem breakage can sometimes be difficult to discern from actual traumatic injury in archaeological remains.

With my assessment complete, I tabulate the data. The population has a total of ninety fractures involving every aspect of the body: depressed cranial fractures from a fall or blow to the head, long-bone fractures of the arms and legs, vertebral fractures caused from repetitive heavy lifting or advanced age, and broken fingers and toes. There is little sign of interpersonal violence or conflict. These contexts are depicted on the skeleton in the form of multiple injuries or obvious weapon-related wounds, such as stone points embedded in the skeleton or the crushing injuries to skulls. One elderly female has several fractures of her face in various stages of healing. Because they are to the face, they could be interpreted as interpersonal violence; because they are in various stages of healing, they could have occurred on separate occasions over time. This is the pattern we see in contemporary cases of child abuse. One male is found with an antler tine embedded in his hip; whether intentional or the result of a careless shot, we will never know. But the majority of fractures appear to be accidental in nature, perhaps from falls or the physically demanding life of Florida's Archaic Period.

Traumatic injuries also provide insight into care and compassion among the people at Windover: for example, the elderly female with a broken femur. The femur or upper leg bone is the largest, strongest bone in the human body, and requires quite a bit of force to break. Working as a medic, I treated many femur fractures, which can easily lead to death because of the proximity of the large femoral artery that runs along the back of the bone. The break of the bone can cause a tear in the artery, resulting in the patient "bleeding out" in a very short period of time. These patients were typically victims of high speed collisions; travelling on motorcycles that were struck broadside by cars or as pedestrians hit while crossing a road. Whatever the circumstance, they are serious injuries requiring immediate stabilization.

When the femur is fractured, the large muscles in the thigh tend to contract. This can cause the broken ends of bones to slide alongside each other, resulting in mal-alignment. Traction, or pulling the foot away from the body, can realign the bone ends. Femoral fractures are treated in the pre-hospital setting via a traction splint, a metallic device that is placed under the patient's broken leg and strapped around the foot and upper thigh. Once secured to the patient, a handle that controls the traction mechanism on the splint is cranked, pulling the foot away from the leg and realigning the bone ends. Traction is maintained on the way to the hospital where the patient is transferred and usually sent to surgery where metal rods can be placed within or alongside the bone to stabilize it. The patient then remains in traction for several weeks as the bone mends.

The woman from Windover suffered this same injury. I've spent many nights wondering what type of incident led to her fracture. But what's remarkable is that she was able to recover from this injury; the bone surrounding the break is completely healed. Without traction, the bone ends could not be realigned; her leg was therefore shortened following the injury, resulting in a considerable limp. Not only would she have been immobilized for many weeks while the bone mended, she would have been in considerable pain and needed the basic necessities of life provided for her. Someone would have had to bring her food and water, kept her clean, and assisted her as she healed. She wasn't abandoned; she was cared for. And she survived for many years beyond the injury. This tells us something about the nature of the people from Windover, about the value of individual lives within the group. Had this woman not have been valued within the society, she would have been abandoned. Her situation was complicated by their means of subsistence – how they obtained their food.

The people from Windover were a semi-mobile, hunter/gatherer population. They lived alongside the pond during the late summer and early fall months, moving on as the season changed and resources shifted to other locations. Those who were injured or ill would have required assistance; she would have required assistance for the remainder of her life, since her limp would have been permanent and debilitating. Illness and injury within the archaeological record says something about the people experiencing them; those showing evidence of healed injuries or long-term illness were assisted by those around them. Had it not been for the care and compassion within the group, those with serious injuries or incapacitating illness would never have survived.

The assessment of fractures from Windover provides insight into their lives. Males and females had about equal number of fractures, no evidence for abuse or submission. The fractures appear to be accidental in nature, with no consistent signs of interpersonal violence or conflict. Fractures among the children were rare. The few present were typical of what you might find among young active children: a twelve year old with a healed skull fracture; the broken clavicle of a two-year-old, possibly sustained while the child learned to walk. Although life for the people of Windover appears to have been physically demanding and potentially treacherous, it does not appear to have been violent. Life among the wilds of prehistoric Florida would have produced its own challenges; trekking through dense palmetto scrub, navigating numerous waterways, and moving camp as the seasons changed would have provided plenty of opportunity for injury. But those injuries didn't keep them from living out their lives. They suffered, healed, and moved on. They were a resilient people.

With my thesis complete and my defense successful, I graduate with a Masters in Science in Anthropology. Step One is complete; I relish the few weeks of freedom before the work really starts. It's time to begin my PhD.

Ancient Bones of Texas

The fall semester begins, and I am officially a PhD student. It's a strange a wonderful feeling, knowing I'm moving toward a doctoral degree. It seems to carry more weight; it feels more substantial.

Glen Doran, who will serve as Chair for my dissertation committee as he did for my MS, has informed me that he will be spending the next few years analyzing a seven-thousand-year-old population from Texas. Since the project is grant funded, it will fund my doctoral assistantship and I will serve as the project's laboratory director. This is a great opportunity. Not only will I be working on a skeletal population comparable in age to Windover's; I will also oversee day-to-day operations in the lab and guide a small cadre of students through the analyses of the remains.

The site, known as Buckeye Knoll, produced the remains of over seventy-five individuals, making it the largest and most ancient skeletal population west of the Mississippi River. Although similar in age to Windover, the remains from Texas are nothing like the beautifully preserved bones from the pond. The skeletons arrive in large plastic containers. But they are not really skeletons, in a sense; they are small fragments of bones protruding from large blocks of dark matrix. The skeletons are so fragmented that a consolidant was used in the field – a liquid adhesive was poured over the bones and the entire block of earth was removed from the grave. My first assignment is to spend the next year chiseling out small fragmented bones from the dark soil. We will then try to reassemble the remains for analysis. It won't be easy.

The next two semesters are spent either in class or in the lab. As the semesters progress, the blocks of matrix yield to our picks and the fragmented bones emerge. There's not much to look at, even less to analyze. The situation is made more complex by the fact that the Buckeye Knoll Project has been placed under the provisions of NAGPRA. In consultation with local tribes, it was decided the remains would be analyzed, then returned to the tribes for reburial. We have limited time to identify, analyze, and document every aspect of the skeletons before they are returned. We work feverishly to extract the small fragments. By the end of the second semester, the bones are freed and we begin data collection.

We will first inventory the remains, identifying which bones are present within each burial. We will then take photos and measurements of each element. Evidence for pathology will be recorded and several lines of molecular analyses will be conducted: DNA, stable isotopes, and trace elements. We have a lot to do and little time in which to do it.

When not in the lab or in class, I'm poring over reference materials in search of a dissertation topic. I know I want to continue work on the Windover remains; that was the primary reason for staying at FSU to complete my PhD. There is much to learn from the population. There have been no extensive studies on their types and levels of pathology, so I take Directed Independent Study in Paleopathology under Doran to increase my knowledge of ancient disease and how to identify it on the skeleton.

I'm also desperately in need of skeletal excavation experience. My archaeological field school merely produces glass beads, ceramic fragments, and those elusive "features" everyone was so enamored with; in other words, a real snoozer. Not a single bone or tooth was recovered at the school during the entire semester. What I need is experience in actually removing skeletons from the grave. But since I specialize in Native American remains, this type of experience is hard to come by. NAGPRA substantially limits the excavation of Native American remains. It looks like I'm going to have to do a bit of traveling if I want to excavate skeletons. After scouring the internet for skeletal opportunities, I stumble upon the Bamburgh Research Project. Back to England I go!

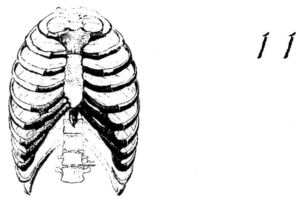

Digging in the Bowl Hole

It's early summer and the verdant fields of Northumberland stretch eastward toward the wind-swept beaches of the North Sea. I get off the train, practically comatose from lack of sleep during the overnight flight to London. From London I flew into Newcastle, located in England's northeast corner, where I hopped a train to the small hamlet of Berwick-upon-Tweed. I have a suitcase full of field clothes and a large duffle bag filled with camping gear. Graeme, one of the project directors, is waiting for me, and he drives me the few miles to the campground where we will be staying.

Bamburgh Castle is a sprawling medieval fortress perched on basalt outcroppings overlooking the North Sea. The site affords many advantages. The outcropping above the sea provides a wide view of its surroundings: a defensive advantage for its ancient occupants. The surrounding lands are composed of rich soils that, even today, support farms producing barley, wheat, and canola. Earliest written accounts of the castle date back over fifteen hundred years, although the area was inhabited long before that period. Originally made of wood, it was destroyed by Vikings in 993 AD and later rebuilt by the Normans. It is one of only a handful of castles in England that remains occupied to this day.

The Bamburgh Research Project is a nonprofit organization that was established in 1993 by a group of professional archaeologists living and

View of Bamburgh Castle through the fog, taken from the village.

working in the region. Each summer they conduct an archaeological field school where participants from all over the world can pay tuition to work at the site. This provides field experience for students and free labor for the project.

Professional excavations of the castle were undertaken in the 1960s but many questions remained about its history and inhabitants. One of the project's primary goals was to locate the cemetery said to exist on its grounds. It was found.

The cemetery is known as "The Bowl Hole" because of its location in a low-lying area down-slope from the castle. Burials took place during the seventh and eighth centuries. Analyses of the well-preserved human remains indicate the burials are those of elites who, although not royalty, probably formed the castle's inner circle. They appear to be well-nourished individuals displaying little evidence of intensive labor. But more on the skeletons later.

The project is divided into field crews targeting two areas: one group works on the castle grounds, expanding the excavations conducted in the 1960s; the other group focuses on the Bowl Hole. I was given permission by the project director to join their project for ten days, not as a paying student, but as a volunteer bioarchaeologist in need of excavation experience. I am required to work at the castle for the first few days to get oriented; then I'll move down into the cemetery, where I'll get to try my hand at a burial. My objective is to get into the Hole as soon as possible, since I will be in England only ten days.

We arrive at the campground, which is located a few miles north of the castle. It is chock full of families escaping the crowded cities, many of whom spend weeks, if not months, living in the campground during the summer. The field school group, segregated near the rear of the campground, is a mass of small, colorful tents adjacent to a large military tent that serves as the school's mess hall. Further down the dirt road are the bathrooms, luxurious accommodations of grungy tile and concrete floors that serve the entire campground.

I knew spending two weeks in a tent would make for the most uncomfortable of circumstances, so I've sprung for my own "caravan," a tiny, lopsided camper located near the front of the campground adjacent to a small open field. Although cramped and smelling of fungus, it is cozy and dry, and the faded pastel curtains that hang limply over the tiny windows afford a bit of privacy from the crowded campground.

I settle in, spreading my sleeping bag on the small bench that will serve as my bed. I'm just in time to experience the exotic cuisine of fieldwork; some casserole-like dish of noodles and canned vegetables. After a cold shower, I snuggle into my sleeping bag and quickly fall asleep.

Because of its latitude, England's summers are characterized by extremely long days. Daylight presents on the horizon around four in the morning; light lingers in the sky well past ten at night. I awake the first morning to roosters crowing, the sky brightening, and the incessant cooing of doves nesting just outside my window. It's four-thirty in the morning. Holy shit.

Breakfast is served at seven; we leave for the field at eight. So I read for several hours before wandering down to the mess tent. After a break-

My small camper within the campground outside Bamburgh, England.

fast of peanut butter toast, we load up our gear and equipment and head to the site. As we approach the small community of Bamburgh, I catch my first glimpse of the castle, a massive dark structure looming against the morning sky. It's breathtaking. I visited castles during my previous summers in England, but have never seen one so immense, with such dramatic scenery. High on the cliffs overlooking the North Sea, the castle sits with its extensive wings spreading along the point of the ridge like dark arms embracing the coast.

The field school has been underway for several weeks, so we begin as soon as we arrive at the site. I'm ushered to the open unit adjacent to the castle, where crews have been working for several seasons. The site is believed to have been the location of the kitchen and out-buildings; much of what they are recovering consists of butchered animal bones and remnants of metallurgy.

The first thing I notice is the vast difference in technique between American archaeology and that of the British. In America, we proceed ever so slowly within a unit, excavating in five or ten-centimeter increments. At the castle, they instruct me to just start scraping and give a holler if I find something interesting. No measuring, no marking. The dirt is dry screened, but because of the massive amounts of material recovered from the site, they have stopped mapping and photographing each artifact and bone.

So I work in a small corner of a unit that spans over twenty meters, my trowel constantly scraping against the butchered remnants of ancient meals. I work at the castle for three days before cajoling Graeme to let me down into the Bowl Hole. He relents and I am free.

We pick our way down the narrow, tree-lined path from the castle to the cemetery. I can't hear the ocean, but the smell of salt and sand mix with the heavy scent of forest, hinting at its proximity. It is my first morning in the Bowl Hole, and I can't wait to begin. Located about three hundred yards south of the castle, the cemetery is tucked within the dunes that separate the rolling fields of Northumberland from the wide beaches

Primary excavations at Bamburgh revealing remnants of a kitchen and work area.

of the North Sea. The landscape retains much of its medieval atmosphere. Although the region was extensively mined during the Industrial Revolution, it has since been converted back to farmland. Various shades of green are separated by the characteristic hedgerows of the English landscape; small farms spread to the horizon. The air is fresh; the cemetery is rimmed by the long grasses that hug the dunes. It is a beautiful place to work.

I am assigned a burial near the low fence that forms the perimeter of cemetery. The grave is apparent; the topcoat of grass has been removed, and the dark outline of the burial stands in contrast to the surrounding lighter soils. I am instructed to "pedestal" the burial: remove all dirt from within the grave while leaving the skeleton intact in the ground. At that point, it will be photographed and mapped, any artifacts will be collected, and then the skeleton will be removed. At least, this is the plan; Mother Nature didn't get the memo.

The skies darken, the rain starts, and the day is abandoned. To make matters worse, our only option is returning to the campground, the

Excavating a burial in The Bowl Hole.

remainder of the day spent huddled inside our tents and campers. The wet afternoon makes me thoroughly appreciate my tiny trailer, even though the rain only intensifies the fungal aroma. I spend the afternoon reading, my small front door open in an attempt to ventilate the stuffy camper.

The next day isn't much better. We work inside the castle, within the stables that once housed the vast fleet of horses that served the castle's ancient inhabitants. We spread out on the brick floors, bags of artifacts before us, as we work our way through each bag, washing the sandy soils from their surfaces. It's boring as hell. It irks me to be stuck inside when my time here is so limited; my need for excavation experience intense.

Another strange deviation from American archaeology: they actually wash their skeletal remains. This is typically not practiced in America. We usually use soft brushes to simply remove soil from the remains. But today, we are plunging the bones into buckets of water and giving them a thorough scrubbing with toothbrushes. I initially protest, delicately questioning them about the technique. They brush my concerns aside and hand me a toothbrush; "when in Rome . . ."

The skies brighten by the end of the day and the forecast is improving. Another long evening is spent reading by flashlight, waiting for the eventual darkness to descend.

The next day is cool and bright as we head along the coast toward the castle. I make my way down to the Bowl Hole, anxious to get started on the burial. But the rains have made the cemetery a muddy mess, transforming the depressions from the graves into murky puddles. I begin to remove the overburden from the burial, progressing slowly through the wet soil.

It takes a full day of digging before I begin to encounter the skeleton. It appears as a subtle outline against the mud; the faint outline of a skull emerging from the muck. The work is tedious; the day ends too quickly. We trek back to the castle after a frustratingly slow day of work.

I quickly discern another major difference between American and British archaeology; the pace. In field school, we were on site early in the morning, worked until lunch, then worked all afternoon before finally wrapping up the day; not so in England. For one, we typically arrive at the castle around nine in the morning, which is basically wasting about four good hours of daylight. Second, they break for "tea" twice a day: once in the morning, once in the afternoon. They call it quits around four. Needless to say, much of the day seems wasted.

Each morning, I get set up at my burial and begin digging, only to be informed, "Time for tea!" Following a quick drink and a snack, everyone gets back in place, only to be told an hour later, "Time for lunch!" It's amazing! I don't know how they ever complete a site! After two days of being force-fed tea and biscuits, I finally refuse and work through the breaks, which doesn't exactly make me popular among the crew. I figure I have only a few days to work on an actual burial and I'm not about to waste it sipping tea and eating cakes. The long evenings spent killing time within my tiny camper doesn't make things any easier. It seems to take forever for the sun to set. I usually give up around nine and force myself to go to sleep amidst the light filtering through my shabby curtains. The weekend is even worse, two days to kill with nothing to do. I take long walks through the rolling countryside, visit the chickens housed near the front of the campground, and read for hours on end.

Tea time and rain aren't the only disruptions. One day, out of the blue, the site is infested with tiny gnats that cover us from head to toe. In Florida we have bugs the size of footballs, so the gnats don't bother me a bit. I keep working on my skeleton, trying not to inhale the little suckers. Not so for the rest of the crew. They decide the conditions are just too life-threatening, pack up their gear, and head back to the castle. I remain in the cemetery, a lone archaeologist digging in the dirt, covered with bugs.

The excavation is much more difficult than I envisioned. The rains have soaked the soils; the soils have soaked the skeleton. It is one large mass of mud and soft bone. I use smooth wooden tools to scrape the mud from around the skeleton so as not to scar or damage the bones. But with each gentle scrape, wet fragments of bone flake off. I've exposed the head, which appears to be an elderly female, based on her worn teeth, the subtle angle of her jaw, and the gracile shape of her skull. I work my way down her neck, eventually reaching the ribcage.

The ribs are the most difficult part of her. They are thin and delicate and crumble when I try to remove the mud. I become increasingly frustrated. I picture what the excavators at Windover must have gone through, removing 168 individuals from the base of the pond; I think of the hours and days it must have taken them to free each individual from their wet grave.

Her vertebrae reveal her age. She has arthritis of her spine, evidenced by the bony fringes along the front of each vertebra. As I make my way down her body, I realize her legs extend beneath the fence line. One of the students begins digging on the other side of the fence; we work together to expose her lower half.

But before I can fully expose her, my time is up and I have to leave for London. Her removal will be left to the students; her analysis, to the teams of bioarchaeologists that have been analyzing the skeletons as they come out of the ground. They've learned a great deal about the individuals who lived and died here so many centuries ago.

Northumberland is the most northern district in England. It lies just below the Scottish border and was once part of the Roman Empire. There are more castles here than in any other region of England; the area was once the seat of power. The lush landscapes have frequently been captured by artists attempting to reproduce the stunning tranquility of this coastal region.

During the time the cemetery was in use, Bamburgh Castle was the principle site of the Anglo-Saxon kingdom. Life among the ruling class is depicted on the skeletons of the Bowl Hole.

Over one hundred skeletons have been excavated from the cemetery. They range in age from newborns to the very old. They show little sign of nutritional stress. Cribra orbitalia—pitting in the orbits of the eye caused from iron deficiency anemia or vitamin deficiency—is rare among the skeletons. Their teeth show few enamel defects—lines and pits that form on the teeth when an individual experiences infection or malnourishment. These were the upper class, perhaps relatives of those inhabiting the castle.

But they weren't completely free of disease. Then, as now, people were sick, injured, and suffered. Signs of infection, dental disease, arthritis, and traumatic injury show up among the remains. Even the elite could not escape the rigors and challenges of daily life. Their skeletons provide a snapshot of health during the medieval period; The Dark Ages are somewhat enlightened through the examination of their remains.

Bamburgh Castle, overlooking the vast beaches of the North Sea.

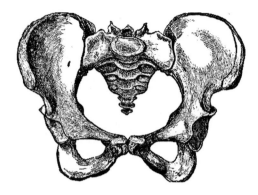

The Fragmented Remains of St. Croix

Coursework continues, the Buckeye Knoll remains are slowly emerging from the dirt, and I've settled on a dissertation topic. I'll complete a bioarchaeological assessment of Windover in which I'll examine various aspects of health within the population. The assessment will include dental disease, infection, arthritis, traumatic injury, and nutritional stress. It will be the first formal pathological assessment of the population and will require, once again, a thorough examination of all ten thousand bones. Data collection begins immediately.

Spring arrives and my coursework is complete. I am now free to work on my dissertation, but I spend most days in the lab. Another skeletal opportunity has arisen: I have been invited to accompany archaeologists from the Southeastern Archaeological Center (SEAC) in Tallahassee as they conduct fieldwork on St. Croix, Virgin Islands this summer. One of my best friends, Meredith, will be leading the team. They need a bioarchaeologist on hand in case they encounter human remains again; during last summer's fieldwork they discovered bone fragments within one of the units. The provisions of NAGPRA do not apply to U.S. Territories, so any human remains I find will be excavated and brought back to the Center.

We work out the logistics of the fieldwork. The Center's archaeologists will be spending several weeks on the island. I will join them for a week, during which we will target the areas where skeletal material was previously encountered in hopes of determining if the site is a formal cemetery or simply a midden, where trash and debris were deposited. The site, known as Judith's Fancy, overlooks the pebbled, shallow shores of Salt River Bay, where pale jade waters break under pristine tropical skies. I graciously offer my services free of charge. It's going to be a rough detail.

St. Croix is the largest of the Virgin Islands, which isn't saying much since it spans only twenty-eight miles from east to west; seven miles north to south. Although natives found their way into the Caribbean over 6,000 years ago, human habitation on St. Croix goes back only about 2,000 years when early migrants set sail from the Paria Peninsula of Venezuela, island-hopping through Trinidad, where they followed the arc of small volcanic islands until settling in the Virgin Islands.

A view of Salt River Bay, St. Croix, with our excavations at Judith's Fancy barely visible in the center of the photograph.

Salt River Bay is a small indentation on the north side of St. Croix. On November 14, 1493, Columbus and his fleet, on their second voyage to the New World, landed at the mouth of the bay, making their first documented landing on what would become U.S. territory. Not known for their hospitality, the Carib Indians – who had already ousted the original inhabitants, the Tiano and Arawaks – greeted Columbus with a shower of arrows, chasing him out of the bay. The Caribs lasted another decade before abandoning the island under pressure from Spanish settlers on Puerto Rico.

Next came the Dutch and the English. By 1625, both were peacefully coexisting on the island, that is, until the Dutch governor decided to kill the English governor, whose people then retaliated by killing the Dutch governor. The Dutch decided to relinquish control to the English, who were then attacked by the Spanish, who were later overtaken by the French. In 1665, Louis XIV established the French West India Company, which lasted only seven years. By 1695, the French had fled, to be replaced by the Danes. Did you get all of that?

The Danish West Indies Company was established in 1733. One year later, the sprawling coastal town of Christiansted was under construction. By 1803, the island's population reached 30,000; over 26,000 were slaves toiling in the fields of sugar plantations. The island's success waned following Denmark's withdrawal from the slave trade; by the 1820s, the economy tanked. The Danes happily sold St. Croix, along with St. Thomas and St. John to the United States for a cool $25 million.

As the plane touches down, I'm unable to appreciate the landscape because it's late and the island is engulfed in darkness. Sparse lights dot the island and the place appears mostly uninhabited. There are clusters of illumination where Christiansted unfolds into the bay.

I step off the plane and the heat hits me like the breath of a dragon. A hot wind is battering the palms, and I can smell the ocean. I make my way through the small airport to collect my things. Meredith is there to meet me and we drive to the house where the team has been staying.

Housing for field crews is hard to come by on St. Croix. The Park Service typically rents one of the private residences that stand empty throughout the hottest months of the year. Our house is a large, luxurious, one-story home with white walls and tiled floors. The interior is completely white and has little furniture. A large kitchen opens onto the living and dining area. The dining table is spread with computers, maps, and paperwork: the logistics of fieldwork. A small area in the living room has been set up as an artifact processing station. It is strewn with large plastic tubs containing numerous small plastic bags, all labeled with the exact location within the unit from which they were excavated.

The best part of the house is out back: a small pool surrounded by benches where the field crew retires each afternoon, beer and rum in hand. I settle into my room, anticipating my first day in the field.

We wake well before dawn to get a jump start before the sun gets too high. In the tropics, the sun rises instantaneously; one minute there is barely a smear of daylight on the horizon—the next, the sun is blazing overhead. Sunsets are equally as brief; the sun dips toward the horizon, then drops like a stone. But the true beauties of St. Croix are the clouds. They are humongous. They float along the horizon like giant white islands, their rims colored in pinks and purples. They rapidly grow heavy with rain, dump their load, and float on.

We gather our equipment, load up in two battered pickup trucks, and drive the few miles to the site, through winding dirt roads laced with chest-high grass. The site is on a grassy field rimmed by rolling hills to one side, the rocky shoreline to the other. Open excavation units are visible as we haul our gear from the trucks. I set up my equipment in one of them, near the spot where human remains were last encountered. I have my tool kit with me; it contains a pair of leather gloves, measuring tape, photographic scales, plastic bags full of wooden tools, and my trowel.

We begin work at seven, but the sun is already high and intense. The site is quiet, the only sound the wind in the grass, birds overhead, and the soft murmurs of the young volunteers who are working at the screens, sorting through buckets of dirt hauled from the units.

The history of human migrations in the Caribbean has been complicated by a primary factor in bioarchaeology: the dirt. The acidic soils of these volcanic islands means that skeletons interred in the ground disappear from the archaeological record fairly quickly. Acid and bone don't get along. Acid breaks down the organic compounds within bone, leaving it friable and easily broken. Weight from the soils atop the bones crushes them, reducing them to rubble. Without skeletons, it is challenging to interpret the human history of the Caribbean; without the bones, we must rely on tracing the origins and migration of their material culture. Pottery, projectile points, and cultural practices provide a trail of human history that can be followed as it spreads through a region.

Lack of bone also means lack of DNA, although we can obtain it if we're lucky enough to recover teeth. Enamel is the hardest substance in the body, enabling teeth to endure extremes of pressure, temperature, and weathering. Enamel protects the inner components of the tooth, like the dental pulp, from which DNA can be extracted. This process is frequently used in forensic cases where a victim's body has been burned beyond recognition.

I strike bone quickly: small fragments of long bone and a few ribs. I work around them in the hopes that they might lead to the rest of the skeleton. But no luck; they are merely scattered fragments. The days continue in this way, lots of dirt, very little bone.

For lunch we head down to the water's edge, each of us jockeying for shade under the small trees lining the shore. The beaches aren't stretches of sand, as you would imagine. They are composed of jagged rocks that spread from shore to shallows. But the scenery is amazing. The clear waters break over the rocks in a hypnotizing rhythm and we stretch out on the larger boulders, enjoying a break from the heat. We talk of archaeology and the different places we have worked. After a while, we return to our units and fall into the rhythm of moving dirt.

Later in the week, we decide to break up the fieldwork with an afternoon of snorkeling. I have brought all my equipment. Mask and snorkel: check. Fins and gloves: check. Booties? Damn it! This will prove a most inconvenient oversight.

We exit the trucks and head for the shore. We choose a spot directly in front of a shallow wreck that lies about two hundred yards off shore. Some of the guys want to try to make it out to dive the wreck; I'm content with staying close to shore and taking in the incredible scenery. With fins in hand, we pick our way over the jagged rocks toward the waterline. The

Early excavations at Judith's Fancy, St. Croix.

guys have it easy; they had the foresight to bring all their equipment. Meredith and I are not so lucky. She decides to stay on shore while I slowly make my way into the water. But the rocks are excruciating. I try putting on my fins to at least protect the forward halves of my feet, but walking in fins over jagged rocks in shallow water is not much better than going barefoot. To make matters worse, the rocks are strewn with small black urchins. The little spiny suckers defend themselves with razor-sharp needles that radiate from their tiny bodies; a most efficient defense system.

I finally make it deep enough to drop onto my belly and swim out. It's worth the effort. The water is crystal clear and full of life. Fish of all colors surround me; a large sea turtle drifts by, his large fins flapping in slow motion. Captivated by the turtle, I don't see the large jagged coral spike rising from the sea floor in front of me. I swim over it as it tears a gash just above my right knee. As blood streams from the wound, I have but one thought: JAWS! Cursing myself for my inattention, I head toward the mouth of the bay to make my way back to shore.

I have drifted down the beach but figure I can walk the shoreline back to our original spot. I forget one crucial thing: the jagged rocks. Although I don't have to deal with the hateful little urchins, the shore is littered with crucifying stones on which I'm forced to walk in order to make it back along the shore. My only option is to return to the water where I will inevitably either impale myself on the urchins or be eaten by a great white. Cursing like a sailor, I cautiously pick my way over the rocks, my feet aching, my leg bleeding, wondering how such a beautiful day could turn so ugly. After an excruciating thirty-five-minute trek over what feels like broken glass, I finally arrive back at the trucks, where I treat my wounded leg and my bruised ego.

The days pass in the blissful routine of fieldwork. We roll out of bed before dawn and meet in the kitchen, where we plan our day over steaming cups of strong coffee. After a long, hot day in the field, we return to the house and unload the artifacts we recovered from the day's work. We rinse the artifacts in a large drum in the backyard and bring them inside, where they will dry on paper towels before being labeled for provenience. When the work is done, we grab our beers and head for the pool. We lounge pool-side for a while, as the heat of the day fades with the setting sun. We then head inside, where we make a communal dinner, turning in around eight.

There is little to do on the island. Most of the archaeologists have worked here before. The National Park Service oversees maintenance of the preserves on the island and is therefore responsible for the preservation of any cultural resources located on their lands. They systematically conduct fieldwork as part of ongoing research.

Each day I continue to find bits of skeletal material; a bone fragment here, a tooth there. The area appears to have once been a midden. How the human material ended up here is unknown. Perhaps a shallow burial was disturbed and scattered; perhaps a small cemetery was destroyed as sugar plantations took over the island. By the end of my stay, all I have to show for my work is a few scraps of bone, a few well-worn teeth. I will take them back to Tallahassee, where I will photograph them, measure them, and compile a report. They will then be placed in the vast collections within the Southeastern Archaeological Center, where they can be used as comparative material by future researchers.

Building a tent to provide shade before excavating the skeletal remains at Judith's Fancy.

Living and Dying at Windover

When bioarchaeology was in its infancy, one of the issues that plagued the field was lack of consistency in data collection. For example, researchers would analyze human remains, yet use a variety of techniques, making it impossible to compare data and analyses from different skeletal populations because one never knew how the original data had been amassed.

The groundbreaking 1994 publication by Buikstra and Ubelaker, *Standards in Data Collection from Human Skeletal Remains*, alleviated much of this problem. Known as the SOD manual, this impressive collection of methods and techniques provided a standardized protocol for the collection of information from the human skeleton and enabled comparative analyses across the country and around the world. When data was collected from human remains, the researcher merely had to cite the SOD manual; anyone using the data would know exactly what parameters were used in its collection and could duplicate the methods on their own skeletal samples.

Standardization is now commonplace within most bioarchaeological studies. But there were still hundreds of skeletal populations that had already been assessed using a variety of techniques. Along came the Western Hemisphere Health Index.

The Western Hemisphere Health Index (WHHI), published in *The Backbone of History* by Steckel and Rose (2002), is comparative skeletal analysis on a grand scale. Researchers from around the world reassessed skeletal populations recovered from over sixty-five sites throughout the western hemisphere, using one standard protocol; each population's health was assessed based on predetermined indexes of health. These included height of the individual (stature), traumatic injury, infection, anemia, dental disease, and arthritis. Over thirteen thousand skeletons were assessed. Comparisons could then be made based on site location, antiquity, and method of subsistence practiced by each population. With this data in hand, researchers could determine changes in health over time, changes based on environmental factors, and those based on the type of foods people were eating. This analysis reinforced some of the fundamental theories in bioarchaeology; mainly, that population health declined as people stopped depending on hunting and gathering and switched to more labor-intensive, less nutritious agricultural diets.

This may seem counterintuitive. One would think that a dependable food source such as agriculture would lead to better overall health. But agriculture is usually accompanied by changes in social structure, and these changes can dramatically affect health; for example, crowding.

If you want to be an agriculturalist, certain provisions must be met. First, you must stay in one place long enough to prep the soil, plant your crop, tend your crop, then harvest it. This takes time, effort, and investment. No more following game as they migrate; no more picking up and moving when winter kills off the local foliage; no more relocating when hostile groups move into the area. You are now fixed to a location, invested in the landscape.

Agriculture also requires people: more people to work in the fields, thus more mouths to feed. More mouths mean more crops to plant. It becomes a vicious cycle of supply and demand. As more people aggregate, matters of hygiene become major issues. Waste disposal becomes difficult; crowding enhances the exchange of germs; more people mean a greater variety of germs exchanged; and the ability to feed, house, and water larger groups poses challenges that require additional infrastructure.

Thus we see changes in health as agriculture takes hold: higher rates of dental disease caused from the soft gruels, made from crops such as corn, that stick to the rumpled surfaces of the molar teeth, producing higher rates of cavities; higher rates of infection, since a greater variety of germs are more frequently exchanged; reductions in overall height, since height is tied to nutritional quality of the diet, which ultimately deteriorates once individuals abandon hunting and gathering; increases in signs of nutritional stress from this lack of variety in the diet; and finally, in some cases, increases in traumatic injury as groups battle over limited resources.

This trend happened slowly, as hunting and gathering diminished and agriculture spread throughout the world. I want to see how the people from Windover – who were hunter/gatherers living in small bands of perhaps 100 to 150, moving throughout the year to follow local food resources – compare to later agricultural populations. Based on the premise that deteriorating health accompanied agricultural development, plus the fact that the Windover site predates all other sites within the Index, I expect the individuals from Windover to show lower levels of pathology when compared to the rest of the database.

According to the Index, the higher the level of pathology within a population, the lower the overall health score. For example, a population that exhibited low levels of traumatic injury would score near 100 percent in that category. Each individual within a population is assessed per pathological category, the scores from each category are combined in a formula, and an overall score is compiled for the entire population. That score can then be compared to the scores of other populations. This enables comparisons using standardized data collection protocols. Skeletal populations throughout the Western Hemisphere have been assessed, and the Index is being expanded to include populations from around the globe.

I have already completed the assessment of each individual from Windover and obtained measurements from long bones to calculate their height. The data has been compiled and entered into the statistical program that will give the overall score for the Windover population. Now the comparisons can begin.

I expect Windover to score higher than the majority of the populations within the Index. They don't. They score close to the bottom, which goes against the fundamental theory of the decline in health following the advent of agriculture. The goal of my research shifts to determining why.

Their overall score is 68 percent; that's equivalent to getting a D on an exam – not very impressive. But looking at the individual pathological categories clarifies the areas in which they had greater incidence of disease or injury and areas in which they had less.

First the good news: in the categories of dental disease, anemia, and arthritis, their scores are fairly high – all of them in the upper 80 percentile. This means that the individuals from Windover exhibit moderately low levels of these types of pathologies compared to the rest of the database. Trauma and infection scores are about average, with scores in the mid 70 percentiles. However, they have low scores in the categories of stature (height) and enamel defects (those defects on the teeth that indicate some biologically stressful condition early in life). Taken together, these two categories would indicate that the people from Windover experienced periods of inadequate nutrition during childhood, perhaps during periods of food scarcity, resulting in shorter overall height and defects on their teeth. Interesting . . .

To compare Windover's category scores to those of the Index, I calculate the median scores of each category and compare them to those of Windover. It too is telling. Windover scores above the median in dental disease and arthritis, meaning they had lower levels of these pathologies compared to the average scores within the Index. Surprisingly, they also score above the median in height, even though their scores are very low. (This could be caused by lack of suitable long bones in some of the other populations from which height is calculated). But they score below the Index median in the categories of dental disease, enamel defects, traumatic injury, and infection, meaning they have higher levels of these pathologies than the average population. Most of the populations were agriculturalists. Windover's overall score (68 percent) is also below the average within the index (72 percent). This contradicts what I expected to find when I began the research.

If general health declined over time with the advent of agriculture, then hunter/gatherer populations should be "healthier," meaning they should exhibit lower levels of pathologies on their skeletons. But let's not forget about the Osteological Paradox.

The Osteological Paradox is an insightful way of re-interpreting what we see on the bones of those long dead. For decades, bioarchaeologists have interpreted skeletons with high rates of pathological lesions as "sick" or "unhealthy"; those without lesions were considered "healthy" or more "fit". But there is one factor we must always remember: the individuals we are assessing are all dead! Something did them in; something happened that resulted in their deaths, in spite of whether or not their bones exhibit pathological lesions. What if the individuals with high rates of lesions are actually the "healthier" individual, since they were able to survive in spite of these pathologies? What if that "healthy" individual that shows no evidence of pathology died because they had no ability to withstand the onslaught from disease? There lies the paradox. How do we know what we know?

There are some ways of working around the Paradox. By calculating the average age at death within a population, even one exhibiting high rates of pathology, you can determine with greater accuracy the population's ability to survive. If people who exhibit high levels of pathology are living longer than those without such signs, they would be considered "healthier," in spite of these higher levels. I think this might be the case with Windover. Although the average age at death at Windover was in the forties, there were several cases of individuals living well beyond their fifties. This would indicate a hearty population, one who could withstand biological insults such as infection and poor nutrition. It might also be a case of preservation.

Windover is the largest, best-preserved and most ancient skeletal population in North America; probably in most of the world. Therefore, it represents an anomaly; if so few skeletal populations of such antiquity (seven thousand years or older) have been found, how do we really know what health was like so long ago, with so little to compare them with? It's one of the problems of assessing health from skeletons. It can be tricky to include the numerous factors that can affect a person's health during life. The Western Hemisphere Health Index has received criticism for being too simplistic, too "black box" in its computing of health scores. How do we know that each of the pathological conditions within the Index impact an individual's health in equal ways? What if infection causes greater health consequences than traumatic injury? How do we discern the two when they are calculated together? These are some of the issues to be addressed in future research. For now, we do the best we can.

Thus, my dissertation is complete. What I expected to find, I did not. The results I anticipated did not materialize. My research continues into why this is so. Is it the Index itself? Is it the Osteological Paradox? Is it the lack of adequate skeletal comparisons? I don't know. We may never know. All we as bioarchaeologists can do is continue to investigate these issues and try to clarify the past through the complicated exercise of reading the bones.

Bones of the Scythians

I now hold a PhD and I am still getting used to being addressed as "Dr." What do I do now? I've spent the last few weeks relishing my accomplishments, but now I face the daunting task of finding a job. I have little interest in academia. Thirteen years with the fire department destroyed what little patience I ever possessed. The job of a firefighter/medic is one of instant gratification. Everything happens immediately: the patient you treat either stabilizes or tanks; the fire you are fighting either goes out or you lose the building. It is a dynamic, fast-paced environment with little room for deliberation.

The transition to the role of researcher has been a tough one for me. I lack the patience and attention to detail required of great researchers; that ability to turn an idea over and over in your head, contemplate every aspect of an issue or question for months if not years. Not me. If I can't figure something out in a reasonable time frame, I usually end up cursing it and moving on. I have the attention span of a fruit fly.

But before I get too depressed over my employment situation, I have two projects directly ahead. The first involves returning to St. Croix to complete a skeletal inventory for the National Park Service's collections; the second involves traveling to a region of the world I know little about. I'm going to Ukraine. The inventory on St. Croix can wait.

Flash back to a month earlier: I'm sitting in the lab, contemplating my rapidly-approaching graduation and trying to figure out what the hell I'm going to do when a soft-spoken student named Rema enters, asking me if I can help her improve her skills at examining human remains. She completed an osteology course a few years earlier, but was rusty. She wants to "bone up" (forgive me!) on her skills, and she heard that I was just the person to help her. Impossible, I think to myself. You can't take an osteology course and be ready to assess skeletons. The coursework is just the beginning. It takes months, if not years of poring over bones, measuring, assessing, and investigating just to become competent. It's not something you can just pick up.

I ask her why the need for the brush up. She then utters those magical words every bioarchaeologist dreams of: a project she is involved in has skeletons in need of analysis. Forget teaching her how to do it; I want to go!

Dr. Nancy de Grummond, an FSU classics professor who Rema studies under, would be conducting a joint project, the American-Ukrainian Scythian Kurhan Project (AUSKP) with a team of archaeologists in southern Ukraine this summer. The site, a two-thousand-year-old Scythian burial mound, known as a *kurhan* or more commonly *kurgan* in the Ukrainian languange, has produced two skeletons from the periphery of the mound during previous field seasons. Rema will be responsible for collecting DNA samples in order to conduct genetic analyses of the two skeletons. Dr. de Grummond also wants her to collect osteometric data from the skeletons. I patiently explain to her that I cannot possibly give her a crash course that will produce any reliable data, since it requires a trained eye and much experience. What I can do is accompany them, analyze the remains, complete a pathological assessment, and publish it! Since I have no idea who the Scythians are, I know they are not commonly featured within American journals. Whatever information I can glean from their remains will provide much-needed information within the literature. I immediately write to de Grummond, attach my CV and explain what I can bring to the project. I hear back within a day and before I know it, I'm on my way to Ukraine.

The first thing I must do is figure out what a Scythian is. The term is vaguely familiar; one of those words that strike a chord in the furthest reaches of your brain when you hear it. I have a feeling they are from somewhere in Eastern Europe, but that's about all I can come up with off the top of my head. I delve into my usual journals—*The American Journal of Physical Anthropology*, the *International Journal of Osteoarchaeology*, *American Antiquity*—nothing! As I suspected, I can find nothing about archaeological excavations involving Scythian remains.

So I head for the library (which I loathe, since parking on campus is a nightmare) and scour the shelves within the Classics section. Classics, the branch of humanities that studies ancient civilizations, is often confused with anthropological archaeology. They share many similarities; they both use archaeology excavations to recover and interpret past cultures. But Classics focuses primarily on ancient European civilizations and utilizes art, literature, and philosophy in doing so. Anthropological archaeology also utilizes a multidisciplinary approach, but is usually restricted to the four fields of anthropology: culture, language, biology, and material remains. Yes, I know it's confusing.

For a long time, the Classicists had little interest in skeletons. Classical studies usually focused more on the artistic material culture of the past: ceramics, writings, architecture, and paintings. I have heard several accounts of Classics excavators pushing skeletons out of the way to get at the pottery buried alongside. Whether this is an archaeological urban myth is unknown, but it fuels our contempt for those odd "Classics" types.

Nancy is not your typical Classics professor. She understands the importance of the skeletons and has worked with Glen Doran for many years. She and I conduct a joint literature search for information on Scythian remains and again, come up with few previous publications, which bolsters her argument for making me a last-minute addition to her grant. The grant will cover all costs of our travel. She and Rema will leave for Ukraine and spend a month at the site; I will join them later for ten days, enough time to get some field experience and analyze the two skeletons. I begin to prep. I gather all the books I can find on Scythian culture. It turns out to be a fascinating adventure into a region of the world I have never explored.

The Scythians were a semi-nomadic people who lived along the steppes of Ukraine during the fifth and fourth centuries BC. They were known for their battle prowess, which combined the speed and agility of

Rachel Wentz

the horse with the wielding of bows and blades, a lethal combination. They were known as "barbarians" by the Greeks, although the Greeks referred to every illiterate society as barbarian. The Scythians revered their horses. Horses are depicted on much of their art and the elaborate burials of the elite included sacrificial horses decked out in full regalia. When a ruler died, his body and those of his horses would be embalmed, put on display, and paraded through the countryside to allow the public to pay homage. These celebrations could last up to forty days and culminated with elaborate funerary feasts involving horses—not on display, but as part of the menu.

Dependence on the horse means one thing: traumatic injury. Anyone who spends their life on horseback will have injuries to prove it. My trauma-loving mind begins to spin: depressed cranial fractures, broken limbs, crushed spines... I fantasize about the types of injuries I might encounter among their remains. Along with traumatic injury, I expect them to have degenerative changes as well. The repetitive pounding of horseback riding can break down the disks of the spine, causing herniations and damage to the vertebral bodies; the knees and hips should show signs of arthritis from the constant wear and tear of straddling a horse. Each of these conditions will be exacerbated by age, depending on how old the individuals were at the time of death. I can't wait to see if my predictions are accurate.

Another long international flight, another long sleepless night. I make my way through the airport in Kiev amidst throngs of people moving in every direction. The crowd eventually funnels into numerous lines that inch their way past scowling clerks who examine our travel documents.

I will spend two nights in Kiev, staying at the apartment of Sergei and Marina, the lead excavator and his wife, both Ukrainian archaeologists who have worked at the site for the past few years. Nancy's daughter Beth, also an archaeologist, will join me; she and I will travel via overnight train to the small town of Alexandropol, located in southern Ukraine. It comforts me to know I will not have to navigate the journey south on my own.

Marina is waiting for me at the airport, but speaks little English, so our communication consists mostly of smiles and nods. She is a small, heavily built woman with a pleasant smile and a steeliness that lies just below the surface. We load my things onto the bus that will take us into the heart of Kiev, where she and Sergei share an apartment with their small five-year-old son. The bus heads away from the airport, through miles of open country before the landscape transforms into the rural fringe of the city. The outskirts of Kiev are lined with drab, concrete high-rise buildings that house the poorer residents. It is not until you reach the inner city that the scenery gives way to the beautiful, classic architecture of central Kiev.

Their apartment is located downtown, a small two-bedroom that is comfortably furnished and stuffed with books. Marina shows me into a small side study that contains a couch; here I will stay for a night before we head to Alexandropol. I have a light dinner and quickly fall asleep, happy to be off the plane. I am woken in the night by the arrival of Beth, who joins me in the study and spreads her sleeping bag on the floor. After a brief greeting, we both fall asleep, only to be woken early the next morning by Marina's small, hyperactive son who proceeds to climb over us, chattering incoherently.

We enter the living room to find a spread of food before us: fried potatoes, sausage, cooked vegetables, boiled eggs, and cheese. My stomach can't figure out what time it is, so I nibble on the food as best I can. It is a relief to have Beth there, since she speaks a bit of Russian and can communicate for us both.

She and I spend the day roaming the city. It is a beautiful, cosmopolitan place that reminds me a bit of Rome in its elegant architecture and wide streets. There is a large political rally being held in the center of the city, with masses of people carrying signs plastered with their candidates' smiling faces. Multicolored streamers are everywhere, turning the square into a bright festival of paper and noise. Beth steers us through the city, to the sprawling hillside museum that houses collections of Ukraine's embattled past: the years of famine that swept the country following Russia's harsh economic policies and the destruction of farms and communities that rocked the region. It is a timeline of struggle and tragedy, the embittered history of a proud and determined people.

We make our way back to the apartment, past street vendors selling beautiful hand-crafted objects of wood and delicate linens with intricate, colorful stitching. We pack our bags and the four of us—Beth and I, Marina, and her little terror—head to the train station. From there, we will take a ten-hour night's ride to the large city of Dnepropetrovsk, where we will board a bus for a two-hour ride into the country. We will join Nancy, Rema, and Sergei, along with his field crew. Nancy will be conducting mapping of the site; the Ukrainian team will lead excavations. I will analyze the skeletons, which will be brought to the farm later in the week.

The train is stuffed to capacity as we work our way through the crowd to our compartment. There is talking and laughter, people passing large baskets of food and bottles of vodka across the aisles. We find our compartment, a small alcove with matching sets of bunk beds separated by a small window. An official-looking woman stands in our small doorway, speaking rapidly and handing out sheets for our beds. We settle in, sharing a snack of crackers Marina has brought along, as the train begins to move, heading into the dark Ukrainian night.

The giant sunflowers of Alexandropol.

The rhythm of the train is hypnotizing, the steady rocking soothing. I see nothing on the horizon; it is ink-black and barren. Residents of the small farms have turned in hours before in preparation for the long day of toiling in the fields that awaits them each morning. I sleep on and off through the night, reading in between. I have brought a stack of my favorite books with me, security against boredom and insomnia.

I wake early as the train comes to life. Noisy porters rumble past with carts laden with tea, coffee, and biscuits for sale. We sip coffee and I stare out across the rugged farmland that stretches to the horizon. The train makes its way into Dnepropetrovsk, a large, noisy city filled with street vendors and musicians. We haul our gear off the train and head for a line of buses that wait curbside. The bus is already crowded, people crammed into every seat, so we drag our bags to the rear of the bus, stack them against the back wall, and lean into them for the two-hour ride.

As the bus makes its way into the countryside, dropping travelers at remote stands, the crowd thins and we are finally able to sit down. The air is clear, the landscape one of black earth and endless fields of sunflowers. I can smell the soil and the animals that graze the open fields. We finally make it into a small town that consists of a single main road lined with small, colorful houses. Nancy is there, along with Zena, the owner of the farm on which they have been staying. Zena is a stout, powerfully built woman with large hands and a broad smile revealing many gold teeth. She laughs constantly and embraces each of us in a warm welcome.

We board a small, beat-up van once used as an ambulance; a large faded red cross is visible on each of its battered sides. There are small benches lining the inside. We balance ourselves as the van bumps its way down the road, finding every pothole along the way. We arrive at a small stone house set

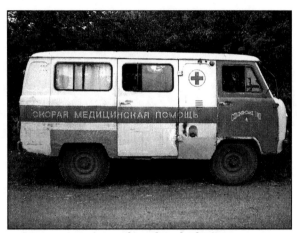

Our transportation at Alexandropol, Ukraine.

on a narrow street lined with similar houses. There is a main building and several small out-buildings, all closely tucked in a small yard that opens to a field in back. A brown barn looms behind the main house, and I can hear the bellows of cattle from the fields.

The farm is rustic. There is no running water; the kitchen is one of the small, adjacent out-buildings and consists of a single small room with an ancient stove on one end and a large table at the other. The main house consists of a few rooms, all open to each other with large doorways. Brightly colored drapes hang from the tall windows and there are colorful tapestries nailed to every wall. Beth and I spread our sleeping gear in the

The farm where we stayed at Alexandropol; the main house is to the left, the kitchen and out-buildings to the right.

largest room and settle in. When I finally sit down on my air mattress, the first thing I notice are the flies.

They are everywhere. They cover every window, buzz throughout the house, and land on us with careless abandon. The doors of the house remain open at all times to let air circulate; although they are draped with linens to help control the flies, for some reason the thin blanket has been pulled aside, allowing every fly within a fifty-mile radius open access to our rooms. The first thing I do is close the drape; the second, find a fly swatter and launch a mass killing on a scale the farm has never seen before. After a few initial swats, I become lethal. I stand in the middle of the room, striking anything that moves. After about thirty minutes, I have reduced the fly population to a few brave individuals and I finally sit down to rest. The fly swatter remains cocked and ready at my bedside; through my vigilance our rooms remain relatively fly free.

Beth and I are introduced to Sergei and the rest of the field crew, several burly Ukrainians hired for their ability to move mountains of dirt at a feverish pace. They are housed in tents in the yard and bunks in the barn; I feel privileged to have a room indoors. Zena is constantly bustling between buildings. She spends most of her time in the tiny kitchen, where she works over the small stove, preparing meals for the entire crew and making homemade vodka. The kitchen is furnished with the same inefficient linens hanging in the doorway, so every surface within is littered with hungry flies. To make matters worse, the outhouse is located directly behind the kitchen and I can't help but wonder how many of the flies crawling all over our food have just arrived from the shitter.

To say the house is rustic is like saying the Pope is Catholic. With no running water, our sinks are makeshift plastic kegs hung upside down from a clothesline, with their bases cut off and stopcocks to control the flow of water. Wooden boards have been placed on the ground beneath them so that we don't have to stand in the mud while brushing our teeth. The water in the kegs must be changed regularly, since they turn into refreshing swimming holes for the hoards of bugs that frequent the

Our make-shift sinks in the farmyard, Alexandropol.

farm. Water is drawn from two wells; one is considered contaminated by radioactivity from Chernobyl, the second is considered suitable for drinking. We bathe and wash in the contaminated water, make our coffee with the safe water. Even after repeated questioning of the crew, no one can explain to me how the two water sources differ, since they are located only a few feet from each other. I take them at their word a take another swig of radioactive coffee.

Bathing is another chore. The shower is located in a small stone room with a low ceiling, tucked between the pig pen and the outhouse (please take a moment to imagine the smells). A large metal tub sits on its roof; it is piped through the ceiling by a rubber hose with a stopcock at the end. It you plan to bathe, you draw bucket after bucket of radioactive water from the well, haul them one by one up a ladder and from there you dump them into the tub. During the day, the sun heats the water; by evening, you can enjoy a tepid trickle of contaminated water that will probably end up irradiating your reproductive organs. The most frustrating aspect is to go through the routine of setting up your bath, only to arrive home late in the day, filthy from the field, to find one of the excavators enjoying the warm water you slaved over that morning. Luckily, bathing was not high on their list of priorities.

The two skeletons I am to analyze are to arrive from Kiev in a few days. So I am free to accompany Nancy, Rema, and Beth into the field and assist with mapping. The site, also called Alexandropol after the small village, was once a large earthen burial mound. Dating to over two thousand years ago, it is now reduced to small indentations in the landscape. Previous excavations of the mound, conducted by Russian teams of archaeologists, produced elite burials from the central portion of the mound. Over the last two field seasons, the Ukrainian team recovered two additional skeletons, both from the periphery of the mound. The skeletons have been housed at the university in Kiev, but have yet to be reported in the American literature.

We all load up in the back of the small ambulance, sitting alongside each other on the narrow benches, our gear piled in the middle between our feet. The excavators chat and laugh among themselves; I get the distinct feeling they are discussing us. We stop at a small stand tucked among rambling fields, where the workers purchase small meat sandwiches for their breakfast. I wander into the adjacent field to snap pictures of the giant sunflowers, which stand well over my head, their huge flowers larger than my entire hand. We then pile back into the ambulance to continue on to the site.

The site is located in an open field rimmed by a long line of slender trees that provide a green backdrop to the site's barren brownness. There is a crumbling stone building nearby, the remains of a cottage long abandoned. A large pig farm stands opposite the line of trees; we are bracketed by the smell of poplars and pig shit, depending on which way the wind is blowing.

Sergei's team is continuing excavations that began last summer. They have produced earthen jars, which provided radiocarbon dates for the site. Just as I was at Bamburgh Castle, I am introduced to a new form of archaeology: Ukrainian archaeology. I watch in amazement as the team of hired excavators moves more dirt in half an hour than an American team would move in an entire day. No delicate scraping here; using large shovels, the team attacks the area as if digging for gold, dirt flying onto the growing mountain of spoil nearby. Sergei looks on, watching for any signs of artifacts or human remains. Surprisingly, he is able to reign in the diggers when he notices subtle changes in soil composition or color, moving in with his trowel to carefully work around large fragments of pottery.

The first days pass uneventfully. Some days we stay at the farm; there isn't much mapping to be done, so we take a day to tour the small village. We walk the mile or so to the main area of town, which is marked by one of the frequent war memorials that stand in contrast to the open fields. Many of the monuments are actually ancient *kurgans*, converted to their present use by the mounting of large plaques and flags. Zena accompanies us this morning, wanting to take us to the small hospital where she volunteers so that we can meet some of the women she works with. The air smells of earth, hay, and the leafy trees that shimmer in the winds that swirl over the fields. We stop at a small cemetery, a colorful spread of headstones separated by brightly painted picnic tables where family members and friends congregate on the anniversaries of deaths to share vodka and memories of the deceased. Zena shows us the small grave of her daughter who died at the age of two when her appendix burst. The distance from farm to city eliminated surgery as an option. Next to her daughter's grave lies her husband, dead ten years following a long bout with alcoholism. I watch the sadness spread across Zena's face as she stares down at the graves.

A Ukrainian cemetery, with its colorful headstones and tables for gatherings, Alexandropol.

We finally make it to hospital, a beautiful small building of white stone surrounded by flowers. We are greeted by two smiling women who usher us inside, laughing and chatting in rapid Ukraine. As we head inside, the clouds above grow heavy with rain and the skies begin to darken.

We move through the dimly lit halls as the women show us the small rooms that make up the hospital: an exam room with ancient equipment standing by; another small room to house patients, composed of two narrow beds separated by a tall window from floor to ceiling; a third small room lined with metal cabinets of supplies that appear not to have been touched in ages. A microscope sits on a small table in front of an ornate window as rain forms small rivulets on its outer surface. It's like stepping back in time. There are no patients inside; no physicians rushing about. The hospital and the women who staff it stand on the ready to care for the occasional resident needing a tooth pulled or a wound bandaged.

The women lead us into a bright white-walled kitchen with brilliant sky-blue paint along its lower border. It is warm and cheerful as the women fry up large batches of potato cakes for us to eat. Zena emerges from a back room, for some reason dressed in a tattered Santa costume, holding a large bottle of homemade vodka and grinning broadly. We all take small glasses of the potent concoction, raising our glasses to our gracious hosts. We eat and drink within the cozy kitchen as the rain pours outside. It is one of those blissful moments that will stay with me always.

The skeletons arrive later in the week, and I begin the analysis. I have no lab. My only equipment is that which I could bring with me: instruments for taking measurements, a camera to document the remains, and my reference materials. We set up a table outside, next to the pigpen. There I lay out each skeleton in anatomical order, record which bones are present, and examine them for any pathological lesions. Depending on the condition of the bones, I also take measurements so that I can later calculate the height of each individual and obtain the dimensions of their limbs.

The bones of the two skeletons are in bad shape. The outer layers of bone are highly eroded, the bones themselves fragmented. The first is that of a young male. Although his teeth are in poor condition and crumble when I try to take measurements, they reveal his age as that of someone in their late teens or early twenties; his third molars, what we commonly call "wisdom teeth," have not yet erupted. His teeth indicate periods of nutritional stress in his early life; he has enamel defects on two of his incisors. In spite of his young age, his spine shows evidence of habitual horseback riding. According to historic documents, the Scythians learned to ride at very early ages; even the women were trained to ride. The boy's spine has what are called "Schmorl's nodes," named after the doctor who first described them. They are small erosive lesions on the surfaces of his vertebral bodies. They are caused by compression forces exerted on the spine, which lead to herniations of the disks that cushion and separate each vertebra. The herniations result in pressure on the vertebral surfaces that eventually lead to the small indentations. We see them today in young boys active in football.

The bones of his arms are also revealing. The right forearm is larger and more developed than the left. This may have been from repeated use of a bow and arrow. Much of Scythian art depicts warriors on horseback using the bow and arrow for warfare. They were carried in *gorytos*, which were hung from a belt around the waist. Bows were also used in hunting game. Perhaps the boy, like many young Scythians, took up the bow and arrow around the same time he learned to ride, mimicking the older males in his group. These activities are revealed on his skeleton.

The second skeleton, also a male, lived to about the age of forty. His bones are also in bad shape, but it's the amount of trauma I see on them that is truly astounding. He has a serious fracture to his upper right arm, just below the shoulder joint. It appears to have been caused by a compression injury, perhaps from a fall in which he tried to brace himself with an outstretched arm. The shaft of his the bone was broken, the bone ends then jammed into each other. Although the wound healed, the bone would have been shortened and rotated outward. The injury also involved the elbow and shoulder; the elbow joint is destroyed, and he may not have been able to extend his arm completely. His collarbone was also fractured. He had extensive arthritis of his elbow and shoulder, which probably caused considerable pain and disability.

His legs provide evidence of riding. His right lower leg is much more developed than the left, indicating repeated use of the leg; perhaps from mounting and dismounting a horse. But his spine is most telling. He has extensive arthritis of his lumbar vertebrae, with large bony fringes along the front of each. This would have limited his flexibility, and he wouldn't have been able to bend over or move side to side. Taken together, his injured arm, damaged elbow and shoulder, and arthritic spine would have made the act of riding difficult and extremely painful. His skeleton is a testament to the level of activity and physical extremes that the Scythians endured during life. Both men were buried around the periphery of the mound, locations typically reserved for sacrificial attendants. Perhaps they had served a ruler in life; perhaps they had followed him in death.

The rest of our days are spent in the field. We finish the mapping and assist with excavations. We watch in amazement as the excavators tear through the earth, their shovels a blur amidst the dark soil. A large cache of butchered horse heads is uncovered. We meticulously remove the dirt from around their large skulls, which appear to have been discarded in a heap. We break for lunch under a small tent made up of sheets pulled across poles. Everyone contributes to the table; fresh vegetables, warm cheeses, and a big bowl containing an unidentifiable hunk of meat. It appears to be a shoulder joint, perhaps of a goat, but the meat is gelati-

Examining the remains from Alexandropol in the farmyard.

nous and cold and, of course, covered with flies. I stick with the boiled eggs.

In the evenings, when we return tired and hungry from the field, we eat dinner and then retire; the men head for their tents, Beth, Nancy and I head to the small bench in front of the house, shaded by the massive large-leafed trees that line the roadway. From there we watch the cows come home.

Each morning, volunteers from the community walk cattle from each farm to a communal field at the end of the road. The cattle spend their days in the communal field, chewing their cud and exchanging farm gossip, I suppose. In the evenings, another set of volunteers open the gate and usher the cows into the roadway, where they are then escorted home. As the cows pass their homes, they instinctively peel off from the group and head to their respective barns. Their behavior is truly amazing. No words are spoken, no prompting with a switch. The cows know the routine and behave accordingly. We sit on the bench, sucking bitter Ukrainian beer from large bottles, waiting for Zena's cow, Rubinka, to arrive. She is a

Learning to milk Rubinka the cow, Alexandropol.

large Holstein who arrives each evening filled to the brim with milk for her calf that waits patiently at the fence on the side yard. He bellows upon her arrival.

I've never experienced the thrill of milking a cow. Zena patiently instructs me on the process. First, I am required to wear the "milking scarf," a battered, checkered scarf the women wear to keep their hair from falling into their faces. Next, I tie Rubinka's tail to one of her back legs, so that she can't swat me with it while I milk. Finally, I straddle the small stool and, taking one of her large, fleshy teats in hand, begin the slow process of working the milk from her large udder to the waiting pail. It takes patience (which I lack) and skill (which I do not possess), but I eventually fill the bucket halfway and am proud of my accomplishment.

We also visit a local farm as guests of honor and are instructed in the art of harvesting honey. I eagerly don the oversized netted hat and worn leather gloves, carefully sliding the wooden lid off of the hive that contains the narrow rows of screening on which the industrious bees create their marvelous

Gathering honey at a nearby farm in Alexandropol.

honey. I move slowly; the bees are docile, having been doused with smoke gently puffed over their hive. I collect the screens in a large container and we take them into a stone room for processing. They are placed in brackets within a large barrel that are rigged to gears and a handle. Once in place, the handle is cranked, the brackets begin to spin inside the barrel, and the beautiful bronze honey is thrown against the inside of the barrel, where it collects on the bottom and is funneled through a drain into an awaiting container. It is the best thing I have ever tasted. Our lunch consists of the rich honey slathered over fresh-baked bread, briny pickles made from giant cucumbers recently picked, and several savory dishes of potatoes and meat. The lunch is one of many examples of the kindness and generosity of the Ukrainian people.

Our fieldwork unwinds, and we spend the final day in the field taking photographs of the site for future comparison. I wander to the edge of the field as nearby cows cast low bellows over the hills. I come upon a skull of a giant boar, bleached and weathered from years on the field's surface. Its tusks are worn, a sign of its age. I pry one of the tusks from the jaw and tuck it in my pocket. I finger its smooth surface as I make my way back across the field to the awaiting crew.

The next morning I leave the farm. Zena's son will drive me the two hours to Dnepropetrovsk, sparing me the long journey by bus. There are four of us crammed into the small, battered Toyota; Zena up front, Nancy and I in the back. We head north across the black and gold fields of sunflowers, Nancy serving as interpreter as Zena gives us the history of the area.

As we approach the outskirts of the city, I see cars up ahead pulled off the roadway. The paramedic in me instantly registers the characteristic scene of an accident and the car slows as we make our way past. A small group of men stand on the side of the road, their hands shoved in their pockets as they stare silently at the ground. Nearby, a small car that horsecareened off the roadway is smashed against the tree line, its front end destroyed. Several yards away, the pale, exposed body of a young female lies face up in the grass. Her face is bloodied, her skin bruised and mottled as her blood pools: the characteristic signs of recent death. I urge Nancy to stop the car; I've never passed an accident without offering assistance, even though I can clearly see that the girl is dead. But Nancy slowly shakes her head, telling me it would inappropriate for me, a foreigner and a female, to stop and offer assistance. I'm caught between instinct and protocol, in a brutal example of the rigid guidelines of culture, as our car continues past. The girl's small form fades in the rear window, her skin a pale contrast against the green grass. I wish I could cover her battered body. I imagine her eventual interment in one of Ukraine's color-splashed cemeteries.

My fieldwork in Ukraine will stand as one of my finest adventures: a glimpse of a foreign culture, both contemporary and ancient. While combing through the literature in preparation for the trip, I came across an account by a fifth century world traveler who described the Scythians as "small, plagued with arthritis, with swelling of the vertebrae and hip problems associated with their life on horseback." When I think about the weathered remains of the two men who may have fought and died in the name of their nomadic culture over two thousand years ago, I am reminded of the continuity that exists between the past and present, the line that connects those who lived long ago to those who learn from their remains today. That is the beauty of bioarchaeology.

Sunset over the plowed fields of Alexandropol.

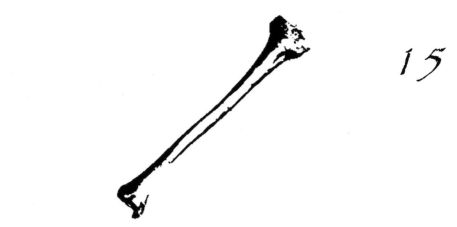

More Fragments from St. Croix

I'm back in St. Croix and it's hotter than hell. I've made my way from the airport to the small hotel where I'll be staying for the duration of my visit – one week to inventory and analyze skeletal material within the Folmer Anderson Collection housed at Fort Christiansvaern, the colonial fort located at Christiansted National Historic Site. The fort, built by the Danes in 1738, is built of bright yellow bricks and is perched on the edge of Christiansted Harbor. The fort and its adjacent buildings were built atop the ruins of the 1665 French village of "Bassin." Aside from serving the Danish Army, the fort was later used as a jail and place of worship. Although outfitted with dark dungeons and numerous canons, the fort never saw action. Across a green lawn stands the Old Danish Customs House. Originally constructed of the same yellow bricks in 1734, the House served as the second stop for merchants doing business at the port. The merchants would bring their goods (primarily sugar) to the wharf, haul them into the scale house where they would be weighed, and then head for the Customs House where they would pay taxes before the merchandise was shipped abroad.

The wharf also played an important role in the infamous "Triangular Trade" that brought captured West Africans from the Guinea Coast to Christiansted, where they were then auctioned off and shipped to Europe. The route would begin in England, where European goods were shipped to

Africa, where they were sold. The newly created space on the ships was then filled with captured slaves. The ship would then sail for the West Indies where the slaves were sold to plantation owners in need of laborers. The ships would then be loaded with island goods, such as molasses, sugar, rum, and tobacco, and head back to England whereupon the cycle would repeat itself. In the two-hundred-year period between 1650 and 1850, it is estimated that over twelve million slaves were transported within the Triangle. What is even more shocking is that the journey itself killed twice as many as those who survived to be sold.

Folmer Anderson was a Danish plantation manager who lived on the island during the early 1900s. An amateur archaeologist, he amassed a personal collection of over thirteen thousand artifacts through small-scale excavations, through purchases, and as gifts from those familiar with his interest in Caribbean prehistory. Following his death, his collection was purchased by the St. Croix Museum and later donated to the National Park Service for safekeeping. The collection is housed in a small climate-controlled storage room on the lower floor of the historic fort. I have been invited by NPS to conduct a skeletal inventory and analysis of the collection, the first ever completed at the fort.

Within Anderson's vast collection are skeletons. There is little provenience information; many are simply fragmented remains excavated by Anderson from sites on the island, their burial contexts unknown. I am tasked with identifying each bone within the collection, obtaining metric data when possible, and identifying any pathological lesions among the remains. It's not going to be easy.

The collections room is very small and very cold. It is approximately fifteen by fifteen feet, is filled with metallic storage cabinets, and has a single small window that looks out over the sky blue bay. I'm grateful for the air conditioning and window; I'm disappointed with the condition of the skeletons. They are in lousy shape. Many are packed in small boxes, most of the boxes filled with jumbled fragments. It's always a bad sign when the skeleton you are going to analyze can be stored in a shoebox. There are few complete bones; metric data will be practically non-existent. I start with Cabinet No. 1 and work my way through the collection.

I am reminded of the harsh volcanic soils in which I dug the previous summer at Judith's Fancy. The outer cortexes of the bones are weathered and crumbling. The majority of them are pale yellow as a result of acidic soils and rain. I can identify many of them based on the shape of their shafts, but with so many of the bone ends broken or missing, I am unable to get accurate measurements. The teeth aren't much better. Although most of them have the characteristic wear of prehistoric peoples, the majority of them were recovered loose in the ground, the jaws nowhere to be found. I can obtain measurements from many, but isolated dental metrics from unknown individuals hold little bioarchaeological value.

Each morning I walk the short distance from my hotel down the winding streets of Christiansted to the fort. Even in the early morning, the heat and humidity are intense; I'm soaked with perspiration by the time I arrive. Fort personnel let me into the collections room, where I am hit with the cold blast of the air conditioning unit that maintains a constant sixty-five degrees. Within minutes, I'm shivering from the cold air against my wet skin. In the afternoon, I plunge back into the heat, make my way to the hotel, arrive soaking wet, quickly change into my bathing suit, and head for the bar. It is located on the back of the hotel, overlooks the water, and peddles my favorite beer: Red Stripe. I quickly down the icy beverage, then plunge into the pool, where I spend the next hour reading and soaking, trying to escape the miserable heat. I watch as light fades from the sky and those beautiful St. Croix clouds change color and drift across the ocean.

Although the skeletons are a disappointment and the work rather dull, it sharpens my skill in fragment identification and will be a valuable addition to my list of skeletal projects. I use the time on St. Croix to finally relax, knowing my PhD is complete, my dissertation behind me. I reflect over the past few years and the amazing opportunities I've had. My training as a bioarchaeologist has taken me to different countries and continents; I've lived within different cultures in regions of the world I knew little about; and I've read the past through the beautiful bones of those who lived it.

And although my education is complete and the majority of my travels behind me, there is one more trip I must take. Doran and I are heading to Texas; the Buckeye Knoll skeletons are going home. I'll close the book with their story, an example of the vast amount of potential information each skeletal project holds.

Returning To Texas:
Reflections of a Skeletal Project

The U-haul is loaded with the bones of over seventy-five ancient Texans, along with the dirt that encased them for almost seven thousand years. I climb into the cab next to another Texan, Glen Doran, who stands over six feet and speaks with the deep drawl native to his state. Together, we've spent the last three years analyzing the remains from Buckeye Knoll. We now begin the long trek back to Texas, returning the remains to their native land. The cool canopies of Tallahassee disappear behind us as we cruise west along Interstate 10, skirting the northern rim of the Gulf of Mexico.

Their story began over seven thousand years ago in a cemetery on a shady knoll overlooking the Guadalupe River. Native Americans utilized the cemetery for centuries, burying their dead along with flaked stone tools, ground stone ornaments, bone and antler tools, and marine and freshwater shell beads and pendants. The marine shells came from fifty or sixty kilometers away, the stone from Central Texas, reflecting trade or social networks. These were a people well traveled in life and in death.

Time has not been kind to the remains from Buckeye Knoll. The dark, alkaline soils destroyed many of the skeletons, as did the weight of the soils, leaving behind fragments of a people. As we head west, grazing the southern boundaries of Alabama and Mississippi, I think about the journey the people from Buckeye Knoll have made since their interment so long ago.

The site, located near a barge canal that parallels the Guadalupe River, was first documented by an amateur archaeologist in the 1960s. It was professionally surveyed in 1989 as part of a plan to dredge the canal that serves the DuPont Chemical Plant where today Lycra fiber is produced and distributed worldwide. Artifacts were recovered spanning the twelve thousand years of human occupation in Texas. Excavations began in October 2000, lasting nine months. The U.S. Army Corp of Engineers (USACE) contracted with Coastal Environments, Inc., a cultural resource and environmental firm headquartered in Baton Rouge, Louisiana. Dr. Robert Ricklis, an archaeologist who specializes in Gulf Coast prehistory, directed excavations. Recovered were the remains of over seventy-five individuals and their associated grave goods, making it the largest and most ancient skeletal population west of the Mississippi River.

Several Native American tribes claimed cultural affiliation to the remains. Consultation between Native Americans, the USACE, the Texas Historical Commission, and the local archaeological community concluded that the remains would be analyzed, then returned to the tribes for reburial. These stipulations required expediency and thoroughness on the part of the scientific community, since the remains would be returned to the earth forever upon completion of the project.

The sun rises behind us, flashing in our rearview mirrors as we proceed west. The terrain flattens out and Doran entertains himself scanning static-filled radio stations and crunching Corn Nuts. The surrounding landscape fades to brown as we enter the muddy flats of Louisiana, the shallow waters of crawfish farms and rice fields flanking the interstate. After a quick stop for seafood-stuffed po' boys, our journey continues.

Doran and I, along with a small group of students, have spent the last few years poring over the remains from Buckeye Knoll; every inch of bone has been identified, analyzed, measured, and photographed. The data has been amassed and will be compared to other ancient populations from North America.

But information from Buckeye Knoll is not limited to the skeletons. The site itself will provide information about the environment, geology, and soils associated with the cemetery. The geoarchaeology of the site will help us understand how the site formed over time. Dating of sand layers will serve as chronological tools, and these dates will help determine how long the cemetery was in use.

Pollen recovered from the site will allow a paleoenvironmental reconstruction of the region to better understand environmental changes that have taken place over the last seven thousand years. The stone tools associated with the burials will also be analyzed. Residue and use-wear analyses will help determine whether the tools were used prior to burial, or were made specifically for interment. Botanical remains will be used to determine plant use among the people from Buckeye Knoll.

In cooperation with the wishes of Native American tribes, illustrations will serve as graphic representations of the finely crafted bone and stone tools found alongside many within the cemetery. These illustrations will also capture fine details that would be lost using conventional photography. These illustrations, along with the analysis of the skeletons and the geoarchaeology of the site, will be included in a final report sponsored by the USACE.

As we leave Louisiana and enter Texas, we are met by violent thunderstorms. Lightning arcs across the sky as rain like small pebbles strikes the windshield. The storms eventually subside, the clouds breaking as a fluorescent pink sun sets over the Trinity River. As darkness descends, the Houston skyline appears ghostlike against the gray haze of evening. The white lights of petrochemical plants twinkle in the darkness, looking like distant cities. After fourteen hours of driving, we stop for the night, rising early the next morning to continue on to Corpus Christi. There, we will relinquish custody of the remains.

The morning is clear and warm, the sky brightening over the barren plowed fields along Highway 59. The town of Victoria, population eighty thousand, is situated midway between Houston and Corpus Christi. Named for the first president of independent Mexico, the town spreads along the coastal plains of Texas and is blanketed by the dry, short grasses of the region. Buckeye Knoll is located approximately three miles south-

southwest of Victoria, near the muddy banks of the Guadalupe River. We can't pass by without stopping at the site where our project began.

The Dupont Chemical Plant is a sprawling, gray industrial complex located outside of Victoria. A barge canal separates the plant from the Buckeye Knoll site, which is a natural mound overlooking the river. We drive down a small side road on the outer perimeter of the complex. A "No Passing" sign stands in contrast against the isolated roadway. A large herd of deer graze silently near a small pond to our right. Ahead, a smaller group is startled into action as they gracefully leap over a rusted barbed wire fence bordering the barren mesquite forest.

The site is fenced off but we are able to see the small knoll tucked under the giant oaks and Buckeye's shading the area. The red clay road ends abruptly at the fence line, beer bottles scattered among the high grass. The hum of the plant drones in the distance, a backdrop to the birds that call to each other across the canal. The scene is a mix of mysterious past and gritty present, a reminder of just how much the world has changed in the seven thousand years since native Texans gathered to bury their dead. After a few minutes, we climb back into the truck and head away from the cemetery, wondering whether the bones are growing restless so close to their ancient homeland.

We arrive at Coastal Environment, Inc., a Spanish-styled house converted to office space surrounded by a low adobe wall of faded peach. We unload the remains and place them inside a secured room until arrangements can be made for their repatriation. The dirt from the graves, which is to be reburied with the bones, is hauled inside as the noonday sun burns over the Gulf. After exchanging data and paperwork, we head to the airport, leaving behind the remains we have so carefully studied. Soon they will be handed over to the tribes for reburial. Our data collection is complete, every inch of bone measured, photographed, and analyzed.

Though the remains are gone, analysis of Buckeye Knoll continues. The potential information is tremendous; their worth priceless. They are another vital link to America's past. Through the examination of this site, some of the shadows of our continent's history will be illuminated.

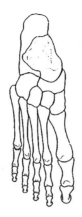

Conclusion

Looking Forward

It has been five years since the completion of my PhD and the events I have recounted within these pages. I look back over the last decade and am amazed by the places I have travelled, the things I have seen, and the adventures I've experienced on my way to becoming a bioarchaeologist. Following graduation, I stayed on as adjunct faculty at FSU, teaching Human Osteology and Forensic Anthropology. I also continued as Collections Manager, overseeing the Windover and archaeological collections within the department. In 2007, I became the first East Central Regional Director for the newly formed Florida Public Archaeology Network, where today I oversee public education and outreach within an eight-county region along Florida's east coast.

The transition from treating live patients to people long dead has been a fascinating juxtaposition. When I see pathology among the bones, I see it not as data; I see individuals who experienced pain, suffering, and periods of scarcity, and whose injuries and illnesses added to the challenges of life before the invention of modern medicine. I imagine their conditions in the context of prehistory – the demands their culture and lifestyle imposed on them and how these demands must have been complicated by poor health. And I see in them reflections of patients I've treated in the past: the same injuries, the same conditions, and the same physical deterioration that accompanies old age.

Bioarchaeology is truly a window into past lives. We see in the bones the history of an individual: who they were, how long they lived, how active they were in life, hints to their cause of death. We can now know what they were eating, how far they travelled, and the physical condition of their bodies as they carved out their lives.

The information we obtain from human remains will continue to improve; our knowledge about prehistoric life will expand as new techniques are developed, old techniques refined. The ability to examine aspects of life and health through the lens of molecular analyses will complement the examination of human remains. By integrating data from populations through time and space, we can better understand and appreciate the complexities of ancient health.

My journey from firefighter to bioarchaeologist has been the most challenging of my life. I have been to places I never would have imagined going; I've lived among cultures I had only read about; and I've handled the bones of individuals long dead. My journey is not over. I continue to explore aspects of health among the Windover population, searching for clues as to who they were and how they survived among the wilds of ancient Florida. But their story – told through the way they buried their dead, the objects they placed in the graves and the skeletons they left behind – is too complex to sum up in this brief work. It's time for me to get started on the next book.